Memorial Book of 13 Shtetls of Galicia

The Jewish Communities of
Dziedzilow, Winniki, Barszczowice, Pidelisek,
Pidbaritz, Kukizov, Old Jarczow, Pekalowice, Kamenopole,
Nowy Jarczow,
Kamionka Strumilowa,
Kulikow
(Presently in the Ukraine)
and
Osijek in Croatia

Written by William Leibner

Edited by Ingrid Rockberger

Published by JewishGen

An Affiliate of the Museum of Jewish Heritage - A Living Memorial to the Holocaust
New York

Galicia Yizkor Book

Memorial Book of 13 Shtetls of Galicia
The Jewish Communities of Dziedzilow, Winniki, Barszczowice, Pidelisek, Pidbaritz, Kukizov, Old Jarczow, Pekalowice, Kamenopole, Nowy Jarczow, Kamionka Strumilowa, Kulikow and Osijek in Croatia

Copyright © 2018 by William Leibner
All rights reserved.
First Printing: April 2018, Iyar 5778
Second Printing: March 2019, Adar II, 5779

Written by William Leibner
Edited by Ingrid Rockberger
Cover Design: Rachel Kolokoff Hopper

This book may not be reproduced, in whole or in part, including illustrations in any form (beyond that copying permitted by Sections 107 and 108 of the U.S. Copyright Law and except by reviewers for public press), without written permission from the publisher.

Published by JewishGen, Inc.
An Affiliate of the Museum of Jewish Heritage
A Living Memorial to the Holocaust
36 Battery Place, New York, NY 10280

"JewishGen, Inc. is not responsible for inaccuracies or omissions in the original work and makes no representations regarding the accuracy of this translation. Digital images of the original book's contents can be seen online at the New York Public Library Web site."

The mission of the JewishGen organization is to produce a translation of the original work and we cannot verify the accuracy of statements or alter facts cited.

Printed in the United States of America by Lightning Source, Inc.

Library of Congress Control Number (LCCN): 2018933139
ISBN: 978-1-939561-64-0 (hard cover: 240 pages, alk. paper)

This memorial book is dedicated to the memory of the Altman, Bienstock, Lowenkrown, Mandel and Mismer families from this area of Eastern Galicia.

Dora Bienstock-Altman and Bernard Altman, natives of Dziedzilow

Explanation of the cover design by the creator, Rachel Kolokoff Hopper

The cover design for the Memorial Book of 13 Shtetls memorialize the life, people, and culture in these lost towns. It is a blend of people, places and things and has many elements.

The background text on the cover is the letter written in Yiddish by Bernard Altman to his nephew Chaim Altman in Israel (page 29). It is a reminder that Yiddish, the language of the Jewish people in Europe. Prior to the Holocaust, there were 11 to 13 million speakers of Yiddish among 17 million Jews worldwide. 85% of the approximately 6 million Jews who died in the Holocaust were Yiddish speakers.

The flower photograph on the front and back covers (photo by Rachel Kolokoff Hopper) blended with the letter reflect the living communities that were once thriving with vibrant, growing, beautiful life. Now all destroyed.

The front cover photograph of a young boy playing the violin (page 26) symbolizes the once flourishing culture of all who lived there. Joy at the promise of a life fulfilled, and pain when we remember what was lost.

The back cover and spine have photographs of people and families from the Memorial Book (pages 5, 6, 40, 55, and 180) blended into the text and flowers These fading photographs serve to remind us to remember those that lived and those that died.

This cover viewed as a whole, is a rich tapestry. A rich tableau of a Jewish life now forever lost.

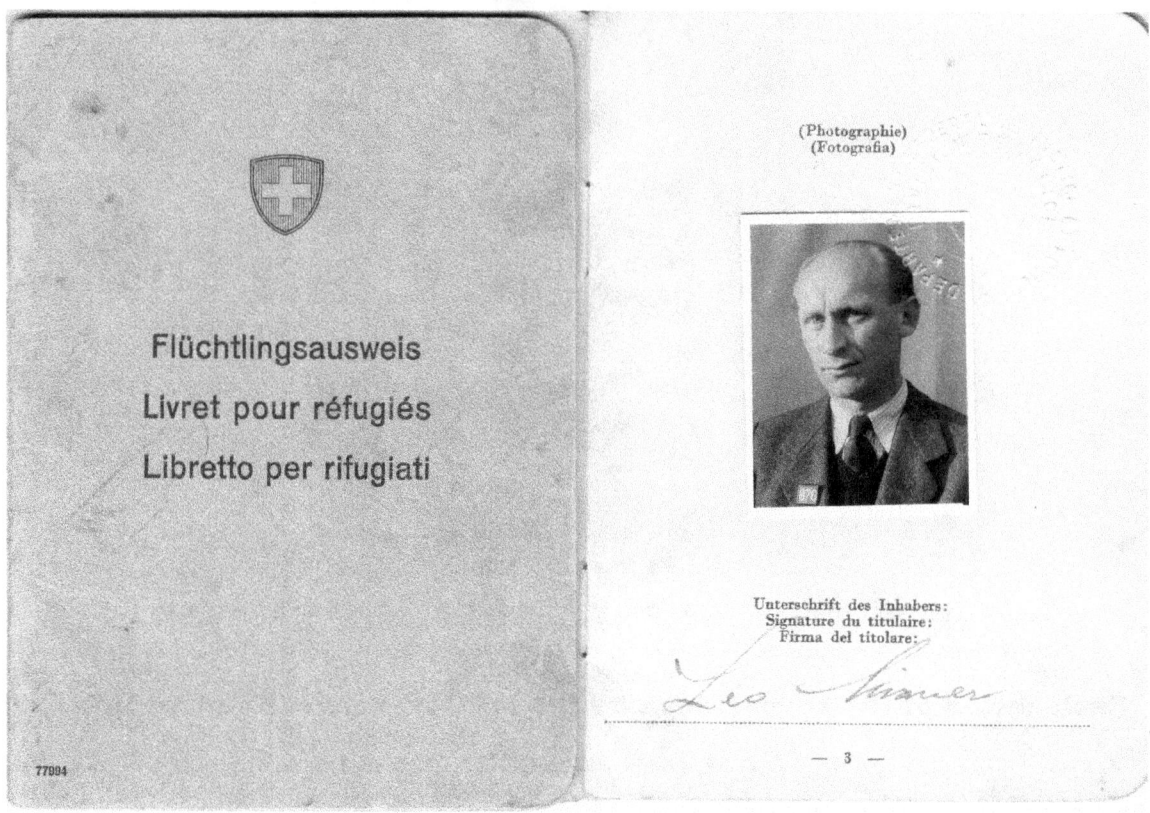

Document was issued to Leon Mismer, a Polish-Croatian Jew by the Swiss authorities during World War II. This document saved his life.

The Germans invaded Croatia and anti-Jewish actions began. The Germans were helped by the local fascist para-military organization known as the "Ustache." Jews were rounded up and sent to detention camps and then to local concentration camps, namely Jasenovax or to the Auschwitz-Birkenau death camp in Poland. Leon Mismer, his wife and sister managed to leave Osijek, Croatia and head to Italy where they remained until the Germans invaded Italy. The Mismers saw no hope in Italy and began to head on foot to the Swiss border. They crossed the Italian-Swiss border and luck was with them, the Swiss did not return them to Italy to face a certain death, but issued the Mismers permits to stay in Switzerland. The document shown is the one granted Leon Mismer. The document was written in three languages; German, French and Italian. The second half has a picture of Leon Mismer and personal details. The document enabled the Mismer family to stay in Switzerland for the duration of the war.

Foreword

We felt a need to erect a memorial to the Jews that were killed in Dziedzilow and in the surrounding communities. All traces of Jews and Jewish life were obliterated to the point that someone visiting the area today would not even notice a Jewish shadow. Yet, Jews lived in Dziedzilow The Jews even had a name for the town: Yidalev.

Generations of Jews lived, created and vanished. No monument for them, no memorial plaque, no library corner and no tombstone. The little information that is available is mostly written in Yiddish, which, unfortunately few Jews speak or read today. We therefore undertook to open a small window of Dziedzilow by translating the nearby Jarczow Yizkor Book that sheds some light on the area. The yizkor book was written in Yiddish and translated to English.

Please excuse the errors and omissions that were made in assembling and translating some of the material. We wanted to memorialize the Jews of Dziedzilow and vicinity.

May their memory be eternal!

William Leibner
January 2018

Table of Contents

CHAPTER I	The Altman Family of Dziedzilow	10
CHAPTER II	The Lowenkrown Family of Dziedzilow	37
CHAPTER III	The Mandel Family of Dziedzilow	53
CHAPTER IV	The Jews of Winniki – Vynnyky	62
CHAPTER V	The Jews of Barszczowice/Borshchovychi*	72
CHAPTER VI	The Jews of Nowy Jarczow/Novyy Jartchov/Ydalev**	82
CHAPTER VII	The Khurban Yizkor Bookof Nowy Jarczow	95
CHAPTER VIII	The list of names in the Yizkor Book	134
CHAPTER IX	Mismer family from Kulikow near Jarczow to Osijek, Croatia	171
CHAPTER X	The Jews of Kamionka–Strumilowa	216
CHAPTER XI	Updated Partial list of the Jews in the areas	225
CHAPTER XII	Bibliography	232

* This chapter also contains details about the communities of Kukizow, Pekalowice, Podliski-Pidelisek, Pidbaritz-Pobortse, Old Jarczow and Kameopole

** See also Destruction of Jaryczow: Memorial Book to the Martyrs of Jarczow and Surroundings

Chapter I

The Altman Family of Dziedzilow

Dziedzilow - Yidalev

(Didyliv, Ukraine)

49°56' 24°22'

3.2 Miles From Nowy Jarczow, near Lemberg/Lwow/Lviv

לבוב מחוז

Lwow-Lviv-Lemberg district. The city is marked with a large grated box.
This is an old map of Jewish communities in the Ukraine, formerly Poland.

וינניק

Next to the city of Lemberg is the hamlet of Winniki

יאריצ'וב נובי

New Jarczow is located above Wynniki

קוליקוב

The hamlet of Kulikow is above Nowy Jarczow

קאמיונסקה סטרומילובה

The hamlet of Kamionska Strumilowa is above Kulikow.

The other mentioned hamlets are in this area but had tiny Jewish communities.

The city of Lviv (Ukrainian), Lwow (Polish), Lemberg (German and Yiddish). Lemberg is the administrative city of the region. It once had a large a large Jewish population Jewish population that Hitler exterminated, although there is still a Jewish community in Lemberg city. The city's Polish population was also greatly reduced following World War II when the entire region was awarded to the Soviet Union.The region had many small Jewish communities that were eliminated during the war

Lemberg once had a large Jewish population that Hitler exterminated, although there is still a Jewish community in Lemberg city. The city's Polish population was also greatly reduced following World War II when the entire region was awarded to the Soviet Ukrainian state. The black line on the map moves northeast past many small villages whose Jewish communities were eliminated during the war. The line passes Nowy Jarczow, which once had a sizable Jewish population that was exterminated in the hamlet itself. A short distance from Lemberg is the hamlet known as Dziedzilow, Dedyliv and Yidalev. Dziedzilow is 3.2 miles from Nowy Jarczow.

The Dziedzilow Jewish community is listed in the Pinkas Kehilot book and is published by Yad Vashem in Hebrew. The hamlet had a sizable Jewish community that existed for generations, as will be shown in the following pages. As mentioned above, Dziedzilow was located near Nowy Jarczow, which had a large Jewish community.

The small village was known by many Polish, Yiddish and Ukrainian names and all are remembered. Today it is part of Ukraine and there are no Jews in the area. The village is primarily an agricultural area and its population was predominantly Polish when the area belonged to Poland; now the area is predominantly Ukrainian. Once the ruling elite was Polish and the majority of the rural population belonged to the Roman Catholic Church. The local Ukrainians belonged to the Orthodox Churches and to the Greek Catholic Church. The Jews created a buffer zone so to speak between the

Christian populations. Animosity frequently ran high among the various populations, especially between the Jewish and non-Jewish population. The Polish establishment ruled with an iron hand and suppressed any expression of Ukrainian nationalism. The Christian populations disliked the Jews but tolerated them. The Polish administration occasionally gave free rein to the Ukrainian population to let off some steam, which expressed itself in small pogroms aimed at the Jews.

A former resident of Dziedzilow, Pesha Altman-Pasternak, described in her testimony pages at Yad Vashem one such painful incident. Pesha Pasternak, formerly Pesha Altman, daughter of Shmuel and Tziporah Altman, was born in 1910 in Dziedzilow. The Altman family was large and extensive and had lived for generations in Dziedzilow. Pesha grew up in the village where her family had a store. She attended primary school but never made friends with the non-Jewish children. She worked in the store and learned to speak Ukrainian fluently, which would later save her life. The basic language in the Altman home was Yiddish and the family was religious. Pesha married Pessah Rozen from Kamionka, formerly *gmina* Kozlowska in the district of Lubertow, a nearby town. The couple opened a small store and lived in the back. They lived modestly and Pesha gave birth to a daughter who they named Frume Dworah. In 1935, Ukrainian farmers began to march to the center of Dziedzilow where most of the Jews lived and started to attack Jewish homes and stores. Pesha smelled smoke pervading her home. She went to her store in the front and saw the place on fire. It was destroyed. Some culprits were arrested and tried but they claimed they were drunk and received light sentences.

Meanwhile, things in Dziedzilow cooled a bit and superficially the relations between the populations returned to normal. However, under the surface the dissensions continued. Jews and Christians did not mingle except in the market or in stores. There was no social contact between the populations, which spoke different languages and followed different religions. The slightest incident could result in the loss of property and even life.

The Jews provided various services to the local population such as tailoring and shoe making, and sold feed for the animals, agricultural tools and implements, etc. Jews were also involved in peddling goods to the rural population. Most of the commerce of the city was in Jewish hands. At the weekly market, Jews met Poles and Ukrainians. The latter brought their produce to the market and bought whatever they needed. Jews had lived in the village for hundreds of years without being able to leave the place. Only when Poland was defeated and carved up by its neighbors in 1872 – Austria, Russia and Prussia – did changes occur. The entire area around Lemberg was acquired by the Austrian-Hungarian Empire. The Empire introduced radical changes, and people could now leave their place of residence and move to other places. Jews were able to leave their forced places of residence and move to the bigger cities of the Empire where they hoped to improve their lot.

Dziedzilow was no exception. The young Jews became restless, including members of the Altman family. This was a large family that had lived in Dziedzilow for hundreds of years. The patriarch of the family, Yossef Altman, had eight children: Shmuel, Mordechai, Luzer, Noach, Bracha Milke and Abraham.

All of the children married and had large families, as the family chart below indicates. All struggled to eke out a living. Some peddled while others worked in various shops.

GaliciaYizkor Book

The Yossef Altman family

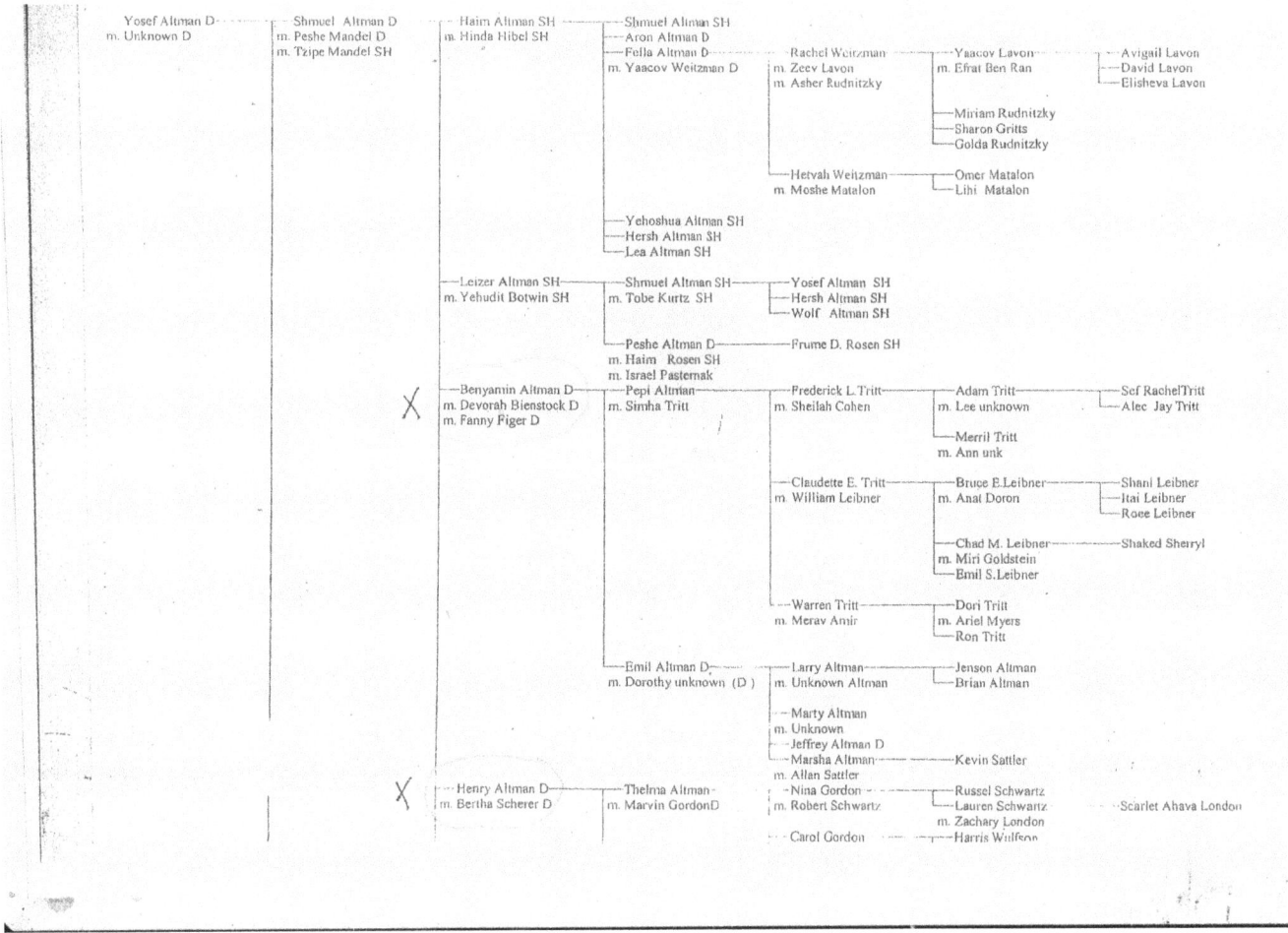

The following Altmans on this page were killed in the Shoah:

Tzipe Altman-Mandel,

Chaim and Hinda Altman and their children: Shmuel, Aaron, Yehoshua, Hersh and Lea.

Leizer and Yehudit Altman and their son Shmuel Altman and his wife Tobe Kurtz-Altman, and their children: Yossef, Hersh and Wolf.

Frume Dworah Rozen, daughter of Pesha Altman-Rozen

Only four Altmans on this page survived the Shoa: Fela, Bernhardt, Pesha and Henry On this page we notice that two of Snuel Altman's children, namely Haim and Leizer Altman perished in the Shoah while Benyamin and Henry Altman managed to flee to the United States.

Henry Altman

One of the first Altmans to reach the USA was Hersh or Henry Altman. According to the 1920 United States Census, he was born in 1891 in Dziedzilow. He was son of Smuel and Tziporah Altman. He studied at the "heder" or religious scholl how to read religious texts. He saw no future in Dziedzilow and left the place. He then headed for the United States. He reached the United States in 1905 and was naturalized in 1913. He lived at 1555 Minford Place, Bronx, New York and was a grocery salesman. He married Bertha Scherer, who was born in 1888 in Austria, and arrived in the USA in 1903. She was naturalized in 1910. They had two children, Thelma and Seymour Altman.

Bertha Scherer-Altman wife of Henry Altman

Henry later worked for the Yiddish daily newspaper The Morgen Journal that was printed daily and served the Jewish population that spoke and read Yiddish. The newspaper was founded in 1901 by the politically conservative and religiously Orthodox publisher Jacob Saphirshtein,. It was also unique in its support of the Republican Party. In 1916 it reached its peak circulation of 111,000. The same year Jacob Fishman was appointed editor, and under his direction the paper took on a more liberal, intellectual tone. Among its prominent writers, we can mention the poet Jacob Glatstein and the critics Bernard Gorin and A. Mukdoni. In common with the rest of Yiddish press, the newspaper's readership declined steadily after World War 1. In 1928 it absorbed Yidishes Tagblat, and in 1952 it merged with Der Tog. It ceased publication in 1971.

Henry Altman worked for this paper.

Henry was very active in the Jarczover relief society that helped the Jewish communities between the wars. It provided assistance to the new Jewish arrivals to the United States. Following the war, the society helped the Jewish Shoah survivors in the area of Jarczow and vicinity by sending food packages or money to the survivors following the war. It helped to absorb the newcomers to the United The Jarczover landsmanshaft also published the Yizkor book entitled "The Khurban of Jarczow" or the destruction of Jarczow written by Rabbi Gerstel.

Yizkor Book Dedicated to the Martyred Jews of Jarczow and Nearby Communities.

The officers of the Jarczow Relief Society were:

Abraham Baum, Chairman

Kalman {Charlie} Shehr, Treasurer

Rabbi Dr. Mordechai Gerstel

Zeev {William} Taube

Haim Eleazar {Haymi} Sirop

Leizer {Louis} Lacher

Izi Stoltsberg

Abraham Klap

Jacob Zimmerman

Harry Zimmerman

Henry Altman

Ahron Morer

Izi Frostak

The society organized each year an annual memorial day for the Jews that were killed during the war. The flyer above was sent to all the members of the society to inform them that a Yizkor memorial service would be held on February 9, 1958 at 2.30 in the afternoon. The flyer is written in Yiddish and informed the members that services for the murdered Jews would be conducted by rabbis and a well-known cantor namely Henry Altman.

חורבן יארטשוב
בײַ לעמבערג

ספר זכרון
לקדושי יארטשוב וסביבותיה

א קורצע בעשרייבונג פונ'ם צווייטען וועלט-קריג און פון דעם
לעבען און חורבן פון א אידיש שטעטיל אין פוילן, מיט די נעמען פון
די קדושים. אלעס געניי לויט אמת'ע פאקטען.

געשריבען
פון
הרב דר. מרדכי גערסטל

ארויסגענעבען דורך
ר' אברהם (אברהמ'טשע) בוים

Cover of the Jarczover Yizkor Book

Yiddish flyer informing the members that a Yizkor memorial service will be held

Henry Altman dressed in his cantorial vestments

Henry Altman was a family man and devoted himself to his family. He attended his grandaughter's wedding.

On the left, Bertha Sherer-Altman wife of Henry Altman, Nina Schwartz their granddaughter and Henry Altman.

Bernard Altman

Benyamin or Bernard Altman

Bernard Altman was born in Dziedzilow in 1881 to Shmuel and Pesha Altman. He went to " heder where he to read religious Hebrew textsts. He worked at various jabs. He married Dworah later called Dora in Dziedzilow. The opportunities were limited in the shtetl so the family moved to Lemberg. Here Bernard started a business. The family gave birth to Pepi Altman in 1912 and Emil Altman in 1914. With the outbreak of World War I, the family moved to Vienna, the capital of the Austrian Empire. Following the war, jobs were scarce and the economic situation steadily declined. Bernard decided to head to the United States where his brother was living.

He boarded the "Majestic" ship heading to the United States. The 1923 passenger manifest listed Bernhardt Altman. He departed Southampton May 2, 1923 and reached New York May 8,1923 It lists him as a concrete-cement maker aged 37. He speaks German, but is a Polish citizen of Jewish descent. His last permanent address is with his wife Dora Altman in Vienna, Austria.

Dora Bienstock married Bernhardt Altman

(Her Hebrew name was Dworah Bienstock and his Benyamin Altman)

Benyamin returned to Vienna, Austria again in 1925 to see his wife and children.

Below is another arrival entry at the port of New York for Bernhardt Altman.

Passenger aboard the S. S. Majestic.

Bernhard Altman

Age 39

Occupation: Cementer

Nationality: Polish

Race or People: German

Last Permanent Address: Vienna, Austria

Nearest relative in Country Whence...Wife - Dora, Obermillner str. 5, Vienna II, Austria

Joining relative: Henry Altman, 1555 Minford Place, Bronx

Height 5' 6"

Hair: Black

Eyes: Grey.

Place of Birth: Dedilow, Poland.

Pepi Altman **Emil Altman**

U.S. Naturalization Certificate for Bernhardt Altman, dated March 15, 1929. He later changed his name to Bernard Altman

In the 1930 Census, a Bernard and Dora Altman were living in the Bronx with a son Emil and a daughter Pepi.

**Bernard Altman's family:
Josephine or Pepi Altman, Dora Bienstock-Altman, Emil Altman and Bernard Altman**

From the left are Pepi Altman, her mother Dora Altman, her brother Emil Altman and her father Bernard Altman.

Bernard Altman kept in touch with the Altman family. Below is a letter in Yiddish to Haim Altman, a nephew.

Bernard Altman wrote in fluent Yiddish letter to his nephew Chaim Altman in Israel.

ליעבע חיים אין דיין ליעבע הרציגע פרוי זאל לעבען

א הארציגען דאנק פאר דעם באזוך ווי איך פיר די בילדער

איך ווינש אייך מזל ברכה והצלכה אין אייר נייע היים

השם יתברך זאל אייך העלפען איהר זאלט זיין געזונט

אונד האבען פרנסה אונד איירע טיירע עלטערן זאלען זעען א סך נחת ביי אייך

ליבע חיים ווי איך ווייס מיזט דו דאך יעצט צוגעהן אין ביזנעס מיט דיין שוויגער'ס פאטער וועלעכער ווי איך ווייס איז זעער א פיינער מענטש

אויך איך בין צושאר דו מיזט צופארדען פון דיין פארטרערשיפ

אויך דיין ליעבע שוויגערטאכטער איז א זעער ליעבענדע פרוי.

אויך איך בין זעער צופרידעו דאס דו זעעסט זיי יעדען טאג

אצינד וויל איך דיך יעצט פרעגען צי אין דער צייט פון איירע חתונה האסטו דו שוין איינמאל געזעען דיינע ליעבע עלטערן אויך

לאמיר האפען דאס יא

ליעבער חיים וועגען אלץ האט דוך מיין פייגעלע שוין געשריבען

אזוי האב איך נישט מעהר וואס צו שרייבען

אין זאך וויל איך דיר בעטען זאלסט איבערגעבען א הרצליכע גריסע צו דיינע ליעבע שוויגער עלטערן זאל לעבען

ווי אויך די הרצליכסטע גריסע פאר דיינע ליעבע עלטערן אויך שוועסטערן זאלן לעבען ואחרון אחרון חביב, דיע הרצליכע גריסע אונד קיסםע פאר דיר אונד דיינע ליעבע אונד טיירע ווייבאלע זאל לעבען אייער אונקעל בערנהארד

Bernard Altman's letter to Chaim Altman set in Yiddish print.

Below is the translation of the letter to English:

Dear Chaim and your lovely wife, may she live a long life. Thank you for your visit and I have the pictures to prove it. I wish you the best of luck in your new home and may God provide you with good health and income so that your parents can enjoy you your bliss.

Dear Chaim, as I understand you are about to enter into partnership with your father-in-law and must alter your plans. It seems to me that your father-in-law seems to be a pleasant individual as well as your mother-in-law.

I am pleased to hear that you will be seeing them daily. Please tell me now whether you have seen your dear parents since the wedding. I hope the answer is yes.

My dear Feige has already written everything that there is to write and left me nothing to write.

I would like you to send my kindest regards to the parents of your wife, to your parents and sisters.

Of course a special greeting to you and lovely wife.

Your uncle Bernhard

The following Altmans on this page were killed in the Shoah:
Tzipe Altman-Mandel,
Chaim and Hinda Altman and their children: Shmuel, Aaron, Yehoshua, Hersh and Lea.
Leizer and Yehudit Altman and their son Shmuel Altman and his wife Tobe Kurtz-Altman, and their children: Yossef, Hersh and Wolf.
Frume Dworah Rozen, daughter of Pesha Altman-Rozen
Only four Altmans on this page survived the Shoa: Fela, Bernhardt, Pesha and Henry. Fela Altman survived the Shoa in Europe.

Pesha Altman-Pasternak

We already mentioned that Pesha Altman-Rozen-Pasternak was living on the outskirts of Kamionka-Strumilowa when the Germans entered the hamlet and permitted the Ukrainians to stage a pogrom. The Ukrainians continued to harass Jews and persecute them. Then the Russians came and introduced a new regime. They proceeded to arrest influential Jews, Poles, and Ukrainians and deport them to Siberia. Of course, the Communist party opened a branch office in the hamlet, as did the Soviet secret police. People disappeared during the night. All jailed Communists were freed, the Communist party was forbidden to exist in pre-war Poland. The Russian economic system of administration was forcefully introduced into the area resulting immediately in shortages of staples and goods. All political and Zionist parties were banned. Only the Communist press was permitted to print material. Slowly and steadily the Jewish population was being pauperized by all the rules and regulations.

Then the Germans attacked the Soviet Union and made rapid advances. They re-entered Dziedzilow and gave the Ukrainians a free hand in chasing Jews and beating them up. Soon the S.S. took matters in their own hands. They arrested Jews to perform all kinds of work duties, namely clearing roads. The Jews did not relish the hard work for which they were not paid and hid in cellars and attics. The Germans organized 'actions' to round up Jews for work details. They created a Judenrat office to provide Jewish workers for their needs. The food supply to Kamionka slowly dried up since the farmers were told not to sell food to the Jews. Thus, a black market developed and those caught paid a heavy price namely, death on apprehension. The Jewish economic situation became worse by the day. 'Actions' began to round up Jews and during one of these *actions* Pesha's husband Pessah Rozen and their daughter Frume Dworah Rozen were picked up. They were sent to the Belzec death camp. Pesha decided to leave Kamionka and head to the ghetto of

Testimonial page for Pessah Rozen, husband of Pesha Altman and their daughter Frume Dworah Rozen killed in the Shoah.

Nowy Jarczow is where her parents were sent. Hunger was widespread and death walked amongst the people, especially the old and the young.

There was no food and people were dying. The Germans continued to bring more Jews to the ghetto. Pesha met with some of her family members and discussed what to do. The meeting was tragic in view of the Jewish situation. Here in Jarczow actions began against the Jews. Some were shot nearby while others were transported to the death camp of Belzec. The Germans decided to liquidate the ghetto of Jarczow.

Pesha Altman-Rozen-Pasternak was rounded up in the ghetto of Jarczow with other Jews and they were led to the railway station to be deported to the death camp of Belzec. As the column proceeded around a corner, she continued to walk straight and did not stop. She walked out of Jarczow and decided to head to the big city of Lwow/Lemberg, but the police arrested her and accused her of being Jewish. She denied the charge and used her Ukrainian to convince them that she was not Jewish. Finally, she reached the city of Lemberg and tried to find a safe hiding place. The local population was fearful and unwilling to face the danger of harboring a Jewish person. Pesha managed to find some one-night stands but realized that this was not the solution. She saw posters urging the Polish and Ukrainian women to volunteer for work in Germany. She was afraid to enter the venture but did not have a choice. She went to the recruiting station located at Piraskiego Street in Lemberg. She was accepted and remained at the Piraskiego camp to be sent to Germany. A few days of rest and food and Pesha decided to remain in Lemberg. She slipped out of the camp and began to search for a hiding place. After several days, she gave up the plan and decided to go to Germany. It was too dangerous to be on the streets of Lemberg. She again went to the Piraskiego camp and was accepted. Within a few days the transport left Lemberg and headed to Germany. It was wintertime, nearing the end of 1943. The transport reached the village of Neudorf, near Staatsfurst by Magderburg.

The transport of women workers was assigned to a big building. "We began to work in the fields, planting carrots, beets and potatoes. The work was hard and we had to be on our knees all the time resulting in bloody and injured knees." Pesha continued to work until the area was liberated by the Allies and then slowly started to head back to her home in Kamionka where she lived until 1957. Meanwhile she married Israel Pasternak. They decided to leave Kamionka, Russia and headed to Poland and then to Israel.

Fella Altman

Fella Altman was the daughter of Haim and Hinda Altman. She survived the war and ultimately reached Israel.

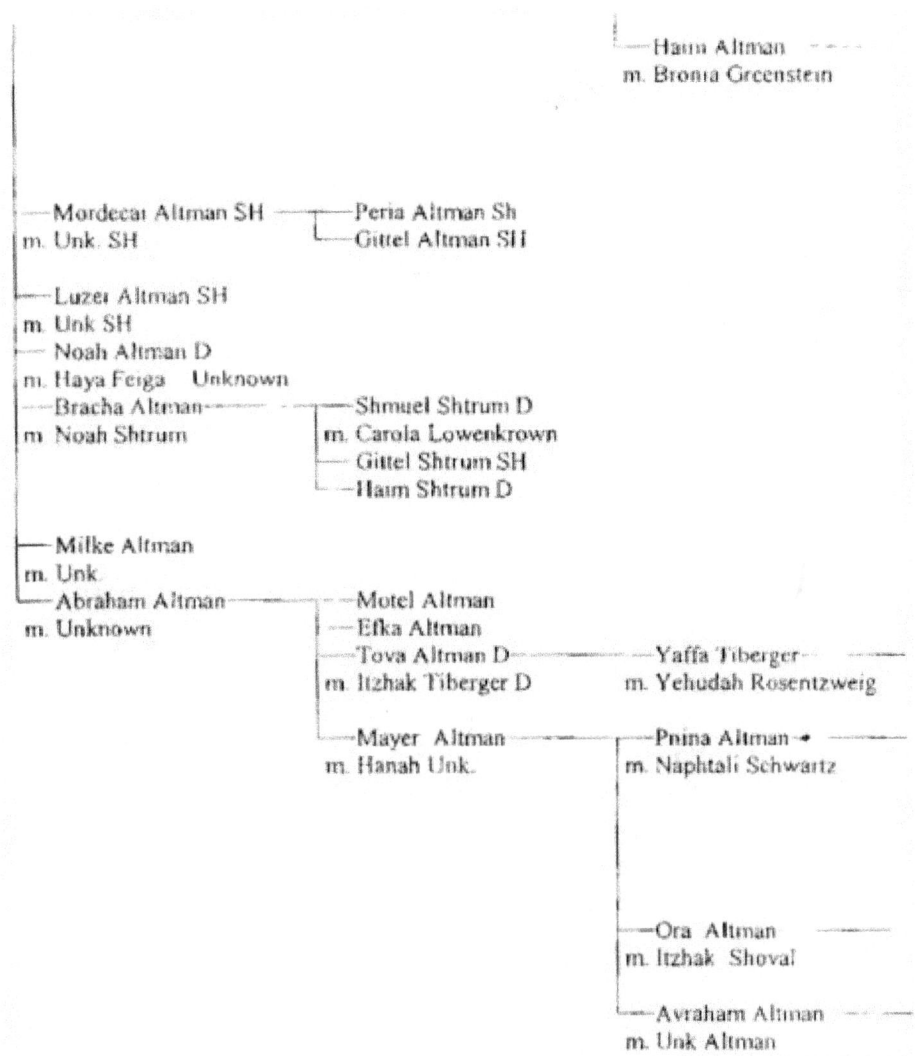

The list of Yossef Altmans descendants in Dziedzilow continues.

David Altman a native of Dziedzilow, son of Shmuel and Tziporah Altman and his wife Lea Figer –Altman manage to leave for Argentina where they open a business. They have Shmuel and Haim.

From left to right: **Bernard Altman. David Altman, his wife Leah Figer-Altman, standing is Fanny Figer, Shmuel Altman son of David Altman and his wife Regina Altman**

Most of the Altmans on thie page would be killed in the Shoa, namely,

Mordechai Altman Altman. His wife and children Pearl and Gitel Altman were also killed.

A similar fate awaited **Luzer Aktman** and his wife, natives of Dziedzilow.

Noah Altman and his wife Chaya Feiga survived the war.

Bracha Altman, daughter of Shmuel and Tziporah Altmanand her husband Noah Shtrum survived the war with thei rsons Shmuel and Haim Shtrum. Their daughter Gittel Shtrum perished in the Shoah.

Milke Altman daughter of Shmuel and Tziporah Altman and her husband, their fate unknown

Awraham Altman a native of Dziedzilow, son of Shmuel and Tziporah Altman and his wife survived the war as did most of their children in Palestine, namely Motel, Tova, and Mayer Altman.

The Dziedzilow village saw a few Jewish Shoah survivors visit the place but none remained. There are no Jews today in Dziedzilow or in the vicinity. The Jewish historical presence has been practically eliminated in Dziedzilow.

Chapter II
The Lowenkrown Family of Dziedzilow

Dov Beryl Lowenkrown had a small store and eked out a living. He was very religious and observed all religious laws. He had a large family that he had to support. He married Pesha Altman and they had the following children: Klara, Shmuel, Hannah, Lipshe, Karola, Regina, Wolf, Hersh and Zosia.

Most of the children would try to leave the place that lacked opportunities. Some succeeded while others remained in the area.

Below is a description of what happened to a Jewish family in Dziedzilow.

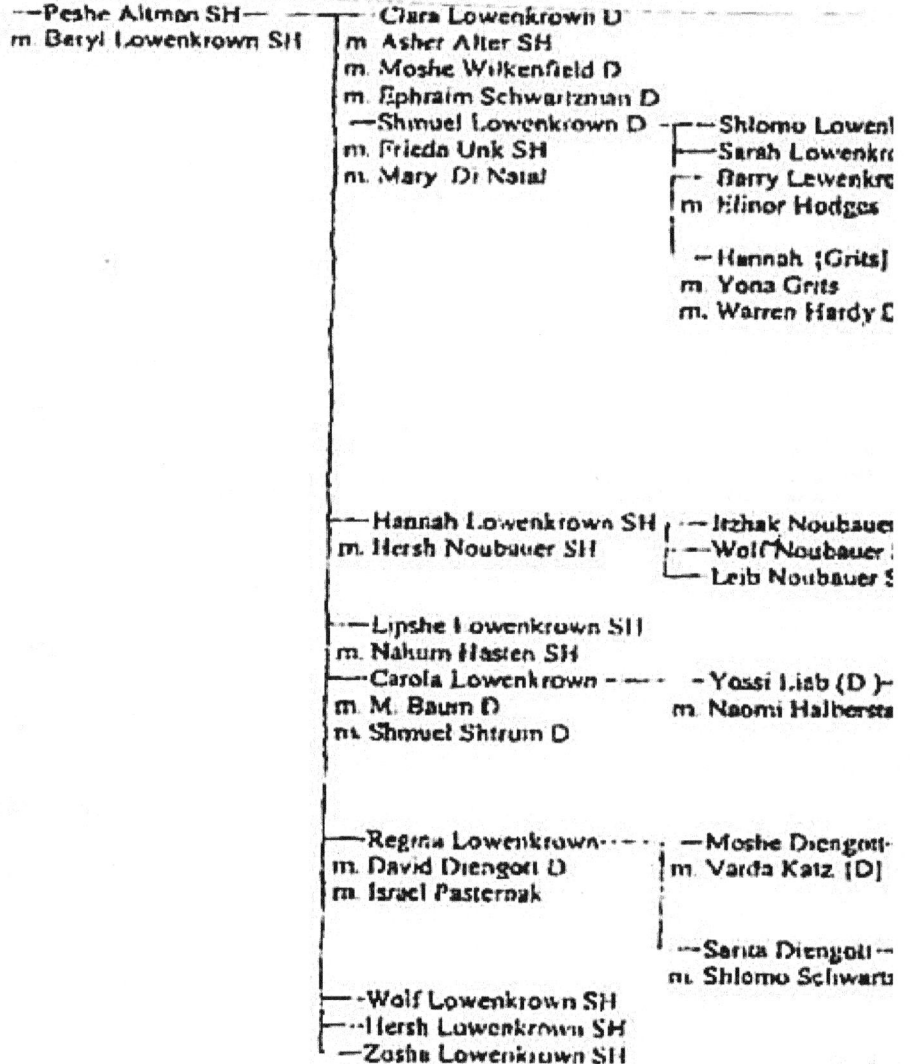

Lowenkrowns killed in the Shoa were:

Dov Beryl and Pesha Lowenkrown.

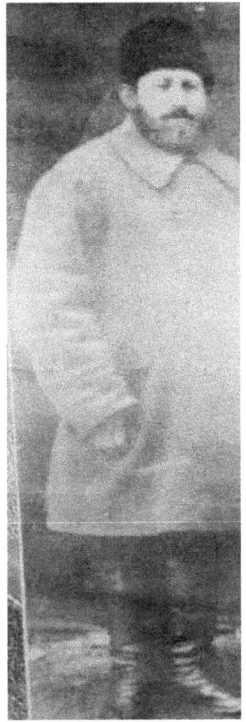

Dov Beryl Lowenkrown, native of Dziedzilow, son of Wolf Lowenkrown, in a Russian prisoner of war camp during World War I

Page of Testimony for Dov Beryl Lowenkrown by his daughter Clara Lewenkrown at Yad Vashem

Page of Testimony for Pesha Lowenkrown, wife of Dov Lowenkrown by her daughter Clara Lowenkrown. Their children: Asher Alter husband of Clara Lowenkrown

Page of Testimony for Asher Alter, by his wife Clara Alter- Lowenkrown

Frieda Lowenkrown, daughter of Beryl and Pesha Lowenkrown, wife of Shmuel Lowenkrown and their children Shlomo Lowenkrown and Hannah Lowenkrown.

Hannah Lowenkrown, daughter of Beryl and Pesha Lowenkrown, and her husband Hersh Neubauer and their children Itzhak, Wolf and Leib. Hannah Lowenkrown was born in Dziedzilow in 1913. She met and married Hersh Neubauer and they moved to Kamionka. They had three children: Itzhak, Wolf and Leib. During the war, they left Kamionka and came to the ghetto of Nowy Jarczow where they were all murdered.

Lipshe Lowenkrown, daughter of Beryl and Pesha Lowenkrown, wife of Nahum Hasten. Lipshe Lowenkrown was born in 1914 in Dziedzilow. She married Nahum Hasten and they moved to Kamionka. They returned to the Nowy Jarczow ghetto and remained there until 1943 when the Germans killed them when they liquidated the ghetto.

Wolf Lowenkrown son of Beryl and Pesha Lowenkrown.

Hersh Lowenkrown son of Beryl and Pesha Lowenkrown.

Zosia Lowenkrown daughter of Beryl and Pesha Lowenkrown.

Page of Testimony for Hersh Neubauer, husband of Hannah Lowenkrown by Clara Lowenkrown

Page of Testimony for Hannah Lowenkrown, wife of Hersh Neubauer by her sister Clara Lowenkrown

Page of Testimony for Nahum Hasten, husband of Lipshe Lowenkrown by Clara Lowenkrown

Karola Lowenkrown was born in Dziedzilow to Dov Beryl and Pesha Lowenkrown. She attended public school but never made friends with her non-Jewish classmates. The Jews were tolerated in Dziedzilow. Jews and non-Jews had no social contacts except at the market or during business hours. There were few opportunities for Jews in Dziedzilow and many young Jews left the hamlet for greener pastures. The family struggled to make a living. The home was very religious; Polish was the language of the street while Yiddish was the language spoken at home.

Germany attacked Poland and the Germans soon entered Dziedzilow. They encouraged the Ukrainians to harass and persecute the Jewish population. The Ukrainians did not need the encouragement for their hatred of the Jews was well known in the area. Jewish stores and homes were vandalized while the Germans stood by. The German occupation of Dziedzilow was short lived for the secret Soviet-German agreement called for the occupation of Dziedzilow by the Russians. Soon enough, the Soviet army entered the hamlet followed by the Soviet secret police and the Communist party. The latter immediately opened an office and registered members. All Communist detainees were instantly released from jail. Many of the Polish officials were dismissed from their posts and replaced by party members. Well-to-do and influential Poles and Jews were rounded up and sent to Siberia. Large stores, banks and workshops were nationalized. Suddenly there were shortages of basic goods that resulted in a black market. All Jewish institutions were closed except for the office of the Jewish Communist party. The independent press was closed. Jewish religious life was hampered; people had to work on Saturday. The new order pauperized the Jewish population that depended to a great extend on commercial activities. Everybody tried to get a governmental job. Fear became the daily worry of the people of Dziedzilow for the secret police were everywhere and had a hand in everything.

This situation ended abruptly with the German attack on Russia. The Germans reached Dziedzilow and let the Ukrainians stage anti-Jewish activities. The S.S. soon arrived and began to enforce the anti-Jewish ordinances namely arm bands, seizing Jews for all kinds of work details without pay. Each day brought new anti-Jewish rules. The farmers were not permitted to bring their produce to the Jewish stores in the hamlet that resulted in hunger. A black market developed but it was very risky, for the guilty party was usually shot or sent to a forced labor camp where their chances of survival were non-existent. The Germans organized a Judenrat and a Jewish police force to provide cheap labor. Soon, the Germans decided to expel the Jews from Dziedzilow and send them to the ghetto of Nowy Jarczow. Old, young, sick and babies were forced to march the distance to the ghetto. The conditions in the ghetto were beyond description. Nowy Jarczow received not only the Jews of Dziedzilow, but the Jews from the vicinity. Hunger, disease and lack of accommodation were the lot of the Jews. "I [Karola] managed to establish contacts with Poles while working with them and they helped me to get out of the ghetto of Nowy Jarczow and to move to the big city of Lemberg where I was hidden until the Soviet Army liberated the city. Following the war I married Mr. Baum and we had a son named Yossef. We left the area and settled in Tarnow, Poland where my husband died. I then moved to Israel to join my sister Klara."

Regina Lowenkrown

International Tracing Office report on Regina Lowenkrown, born February 7, 1925, in Dziedzilow to Dov Beryl and Pesha Lowenkrown

Regina Lowenkrown was born in Dziedzilow to Dov Beryl and Pesha Lowenkrown. Her childhood was similar to that of her sister Karola. They shared the same hiding place during the war in Lemberg after escaping from the ghetto of Nowy Jarczow in 1943. She hid until the area was liberated by the Soviet army in 1944. She met David Diengott and they decided to marry. They took advantage of their Polish citizenship and left the Soviet area of Lemberg for Lodz in Poland. They soon left Lodz and headed to Rzeszow, Poland with the Brichah. Rzeszow was the assembly point for crossing illegally to Czechoslovakia and then to Bucharest, Romania where they hoped to take a boat to Palestine. But there were no ships heading to Palestine for the Russian fleet closed the main port of Constanza to private shipping. They continued their journey with the Brichah to Yugoslavia. Meanwhile they contacted their family in Argentina to help them reach that country. In 1948, Regina finally reached Argentina.

According to this document, Regina Lewenkrown left Lemberg in 1945 and headed to Lodz, Pland. She married David Diengott. They left Lodz for Rzeszow, then went to Bucharest, Romania. They continued to Yugoslavia and then to Argentina.

Wolf Lowenkrown, son of Dov Beryl and Pesha Lowenkrown was also in the ghetto of Nowy Jarczow and was sent to the death camp of Belzec

Yente Lowenkrown, Dov Beryl's sister, with her fiancé Michael. Dov Beryl Lowenkrown had sisters and brothers in Dziedzilow. Above, his sister Yente.

Pesha Altman-Lowenkrown and her son Shmuel

Chapter III

The Mandel Family of Dziedzilow

The Mandel family was well established in Dziedzilow. Wolf Mandel (son of David) was a small retailer and he married Liba Weintraub. They had six daughters: Pesha, Hannah, Dworah, Rivkah, Malka, and Cipe. All daughters married and had families. Pesha married Shmuel Altman, and after her death, her sister Cipe married Shmuel.

Cipe and Shmuel Altman had several children namely Awraham, Milke, and Bracha.

When Shmuel Altman died, Cipe was pregnant but she did not publicise the event. Apparently it was not visible. She decided to marry in order to provide a father for the expected child. She married Awraham Altholtz. The marriage lasted several weeks and ended in divorce. She gave birth to a son and named him Shmuel Mandel – Shmuel in memory of her late husband. She also resumed her maiden name Mandel.

Tziporah Mandel–Altman married Awraham Altholtz in Dziedzilow

Cipe remained in Dziedzilow and witnessed the German occupation of the village that lasted a short period of time. Then the Soviet forces entered the hamlet and established a communist regime. Many influential or well–to–do Jews and non–Jews were arrested and deported without any notice to their families. Private business enterprises were slowly liquidated. The press was curtailed to a minimum according to Karola Lowenkrown.[1] Then the Germans attacked the Soviet Union and Germans entered Dziedzilow. Persecutions of Jews began instantly. The Ukrainians did not have to get permission to harass the local Jews. Orders and more orders were issued aimed at pauperizing the Jewish population. Jewish trade was eliminated. Men were seized to do hard labour for which they were not paid. Then the Germans decided to expel all the Jews from Dziedzilow. Old and young, sick and healthy were forced to march to the ghetto of Nowy Jarczow where they all perished. According to the late Karola Lowenkrown, Tziporah (Cipe) was killed in 1942 in Jarczow. The date is substantiated by Pesil Pasternak in his Page of Testimony at Yad Vashem.

Page of Testimony at Yad Vashem for Cipe Mandel–Altman who was born in Dziedzilow in 1872 to Wolf and Luba Mandel

Shmuel Mandel grew up in Dziedzilow. He married Feige Weintraub and they decided to leave Dziedzilow for Argentina.

They had the following children:

Chaim, Shaul, Aida and Mindel

Chaim and Aida became medical doctors and both live in Israel as does Mindel. Shaul remained in Argentina.

List of Jews from Dziedzilow mentioned in the Jarczow Yizkor Book by Rabbi Mordechai Gerstler who perished in the Shoa.

Last name	First name	Father	Mother	Gender	Spouse	Children
ALTMANN	Leizer	Shmuel	Pesha	M		
ALTMANN	Hudes			F		
ALTMANN	Leizer	Shmuel	Pesha	M		
ALTMANN	Hudes			F		3
BUBER	Haya			F		
GELBER	Awraham			M		
GELBER	Miriam			F		2
GELBER	Israel			F		
GELBER	Henia			M		1
GITER	Yossef			F		
GITER	Libe			F	Yossef	3
GRUBER	Riwkah			F		
GRUBER	Haya			F		
HASTEN	Gitele			F		
HASTEN	Shaul	Gitele		M		
HASTEN	Shamai	Gitele		M		
HASTEN	Menachem	Gitele		M		
HASTEN	Nahum	Gitele		M		
HASTEN	Lipshe			F	Nahum	
KRIEG	Dawid			M		
KRIEG	Riwtche			F	Dawid	2

KURTZ	Sarah			F		
LEITER	Yaakow			M		
LEITER	Rachel			Â	Yaakow	2
LEITER	Yehudah			M		
LEITER	Hatchi			F	Yehuda	
LEITER	son	Hatchi		M		
LOWENKRON	Berl	Wolf		M		
LOWENKRON	Wolf	Berl	Peshe	M		2
LOWENKRON	Hersh	Berl	Peshe	M		2
LOWENKRON	Zoshe	Berl	Peshe	F		
ROZEN	Frume	Pessah	Pesha	F		
LOWENKRON	Shlomo			M		
LOWENKRON	Mindel			F		
LOWENKRON	Miriam			F		
LINDER	Feige			F		
MANDEL	Yentche			F	Shmuel	7
MANDEL	Shmuel			M		
MANDEL	Taube			F	Shmuel	3
MENDELOWICZ	Itche			M		
MENDELOWICZ	Yehudit			M		
MENDELOWICZ	Berish			M		
MENDELOWICZ	Hanah			F	Berish	
MENDELOWICZ	Deworah			F	Israel L	
MENDELOWICZ	Israel Leib			F		
MENDELOWICZ	Malka			M	Israel L	
MENDELOWICZ	Dworah			F	Shmuel	
ROSEN	Pessah			M		1
TENENBAUM	Yakum			M		
TENENBAUM	Tcheitel			M	Yakum	
TENENBAUM	Haim			F		
TENENBAUM	Golde			M	Haim	3
TENENBAUM	Yossef			F		

TENENBAUM	Hannah			F	Yossef	2 daughters
TENENBAUM	Yaakow	Yossef	Hanna	F		
TENENBAUM	Hersh	Yossef	Hanna	M		
TENENBAUM	Nachman			M		
TENENBAUM	Hannah			F	Nachman	2
TENENBAUM	son	Nachman	Hanna	M		
TENENBAUM	wife			F		3
TENENBAUM	son	Nachman	Hanna	M		
TENENBAUM	wife	Yossef		F		2
TENENBAUM	Mordechai	Yossef	Hanna	M		
TENENBAUM	Yuta			M	Mordec	4
TZWERLING	Perie			F		4
WEINTRAUB	Aaron Itzh			M		
WEINTRAUB	Rachel			F	Aaron	
TENENBAUM	wife			F		2
TENENBAUM	Yaakov			M		
TZWERLING	Ferie			F		4

GaliciaYizkor Book

List of Dziedzilow Jews that was established by the author's research in interviews, archives and various lists

Last name	First name(s)	Maiden name	Father	Mother	Gender	Spouse	Children	Disposition
ALTER	Moshe				M			Shoa
ALTMANN	Shmuel				M		3 sons	Died
ALTMANN	Peshe	MANDEL			F			Died
ALTMANN	Haim		Shmuel	Peshe	M			Shoa
ALTMANN	Hinda	HIBEL			F	Haim		Shoa
ALTMANN	Shmuel		Haim	Hinda	M			Shoa
ALTMANN	Aaron		Haim	Hinda	M			Shoa
ALTMANN	Fela		Haim	Hinda	F			
ALTMANN	Yehoshua		Haim	Hinda	M			Shoa
ALTMANN	Hersh		Haim	Hinda	M			Shoa
ALTMANN	Leah		Haim	Hinda	F			Shoa
ALTMANN	Taube	KURTZ			F			Shoa
ALTMANN	Yossef		Shmuel	Taube	M			Shoa
ALTMANN	Hersh		Shmuel	Taube	M			Shoa
ALTMANN	Wolf		Shmuel	Taube	M			Shoa
ALTMANN	Peshe		Leizer	Hudes	F			Survived
ALTMANN	Benyamin		Shmuel	Peshe	M			Survived
ALTMANN	Deworah	BIENSTOCK			F	Benyamin		Survived
ALTMANN	Josephine		Benyamin	Deworah	F			Survived
ALTMANN	Emil		Benyamin		M			Survived
ALTMANN	Hersh		Shmuel	Tzipe	M			Survived
ALTMANN	Berta	SHERER			F	Hersh		Survived
ALTMANN	Thelma		Hersh	Berta	F			Survived
ALTMANN	Seymor		Hersh	Berta	M			Survived
ALTMANN	Peshe				F			Shoa

Surname	Given Name	Maiden Name	Father	Mother	Sex	Spouse		Fate
ALTMANN	Dawid				M			Survived
ALTMANN	Leah	FIGGER			F	Dawid		Survived
ALTMANN	Joseph		Dawid	Leah	M			Survived
ALTMANN	Shmuel		Dawid	Leah	M			Survived
ALTMANN	Haim		Dawid	Leah	M			Survived
ALTMAN	David				M			Shoa
BUBER	Itzhak				M			Shoa
BUBER	Deworah				F	Itzhak		Shoa
BUBER	Shmuel		Itzhak	Dewor	M			Shoa
BUBER	Lea		Itzhak	Dewor	F			Shoa
DIENGOTT	Dawid				M			Survived
LOWENKRON	Wolf				M			Shoa
LOWENKRON	unk				F	Wolf		Shoa
LOWENKRON	Clara		Berl	Peshe	F			Survived
LOWENKRON	Frieda				F	Shmuel		Shoa
LOWENKRON	Hannah		Berl	Peshe	F			Shoa
LOWENKRON	Lipshe		Berl	Peshe	F			Shoa
LOWENKRON	Karola		Berl	Peshe	F			Survived
LOWENKRON	Regine		Berl	Peshe	F			Survived
LOWENKRON	Sarah		Shmuel	Frieda	F			Shoa
LOWENKRON	Yenta		Wolf	unk	F			Shoa
LOWENKRON	Zelda		Wolf	unk	F			Shoa
ROZEN	Pessah				M			Shoa
ROZEN	Pesha	LOWENKROW			F	Pessah		
MANDEL	Wolf				M			Shoa
MANDEL	Liba	WEINTRAUB			F	Wolf		Shoa
MANDEL	Hannah		Wolf	Liba	F			Shoa
MANDEL	Deworah		Wolf	Liba	F			Shoa
MANDEL	Riwkah		Wolf	Liba	F			Shoa
MANDEL	Malka		Wolf	Liba	F			Shoa
MANDEL	Tzipe		Wolf	Liba	F			Shoa
MANDEL	Shmuel		Shmuel	Tzipe	M			Survived

MANDEL	Feige	WEINTRAUB			F	Shmuel		Survived
MENDELOWICZ	Shmuel				M			Shoa
MENDELOWICZ	Dawid		Shmuel	Dwora	M			Shoa
MENDELOWICZ	Haya		Shmuel	Dwora	F			Shoa
MENDELOWIC	Itzhak		Shmuel	Dwora	M			Shoa
NEUBAUER	Itzhak		Hersh	Hanna	M			Shoa
NEUBAUER	Wolf		Hersh	Hanna	M			Shoa
NEUBAUER	Leib		Hersh	Hanna	M			Shoa
ROZEN	Frume D		Pessah	Peshe	F			Shoa
TENENBAUM	Tzeitel				F	Yaakov		Shoa
TENENBAUM	Chaim		Yaakov	Tzeitel	M			Shoa
TENENBAUM	Golda				F	Chaim	3	Shoa
WEINTRUIB	Aron Itz				M			Shoa

Translator's Footnote

1. William Leibner interviewed Karola Lowenkrown–Baum

Chapter IV
The Jews of Winniki – Vynnyky

(Vynnyky, Ukraine)

49°49' / 24°06'

11.3 miles from Nowy Jarczow

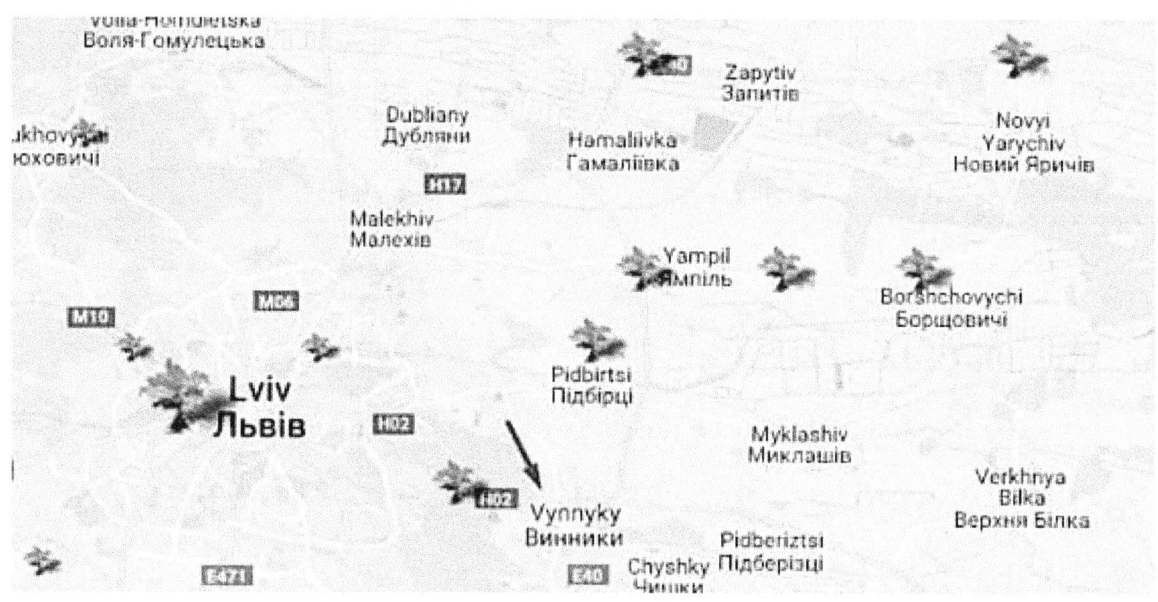

Lviv (Lwow), big city center Vynnyky (Winniki) is south of the city of Lviv in the map above Novyy Yarychiv (Nowy Jarczow) is north of Lviv

Winniki was mentioned as a village as early as the 15th century. In the 19th century, a tobacco plant and a yeast factory were established there. The local population worked in the factories or in agriculture. Winniki is about eight kilometers from Lemberg (Lwow) and provided the city with its products. The Jewish population was small and consisted of about 40 to 50 families. According to the census of 1925, the town had a population of 5,000 of whom 3,300 were Poles, 2,150 were Ukrainians, 300 were Jews and 200 were Germans.

For the Jewish community of Winniki, there was only a religious slaughterer in the hamlet. The Jewish community of Lemberg ran the community of Winniki and provided burial services. The Jews dealt in business and peddling. A charity fund was established in 1928 to help the Jewish merchants and craftsmen with small non-interest loans. Zionism penetrated Winniki and the Betar youth movement opened a branch.

Winniki was occupied by the Soviets in accordance with the Ribbentrop-Molotov agreement. Many well-to-do Jews were ordered to leave Lemberg by the Soviets. Some of them settled in Winniki, whose Jewish population rose to about 500 people. The Soviets proceeded to arrest influential Jews, Poles and Ukrainians and deported them to Siberia.[1] Of course, the Communist Party opened a branch office in the hamlet as did the Soviet secret police. People disappeared during the night. All jailed communists were freed (the Communist Party had been forbidden to exist in pre-war Poland). The Soviet economic system of administration was forcefully introduced into the area, resulting immediately in shortages of staples and goods. All political parties and Zionist parties were banned. Only the Communist press was permitted to print material. Slowly and steadily the Jewish population was being pauperized by all the rules and regulations.

The Germans attacked the Soviet Union and the hamlet of Winniki was occupied on June 29, 1941. They permitted the Ukrainian population to stage a violent pogrom that resulted in Jewish deaths and a great deal of commercial damage. German soldiers helped themselves to some of the spoils. Then the Germans began to grab Jews for work details without feeding them. Several weeks later all Jewish males were ordered to present themselves in front of the Jewish community office. They were told to bring work tools and food. They were marched out of Winniki, escorted by the local fire brigade band that played Polish marching songs. They walked to Piaski, about seven kilometers from Winniki. There they were ordered to dig ditches, disrobe and were shot by the Ukrainian police.

A few Jewish men still survived in Winniki as well as all the women and children. They were moved to a temporary ghetto where a Judenrat office functioned. Toward the end of 1941, a Jewish forced labor camp was established in Winniki that contained several hundred Jews from Lemberg, Sokal, Jarczow and the remnants of Winniki. They built or fixed roads and repaired tracks. Their conditions were abysmal. They pleaded with the Jarczow Judenrat office to send them some food. The work camp maintained a strict regime with daily roll calls. The exhausted or sick Jewish workers were usually shot following the daily roll call. The Winniki ghetto was liquidated in the early part of 1942 when Ukrainian policemen surrounded the area and Jewish inhabitants, mostly women and children, were forced to mount trucks that took them to an unknown destination, probably the Piaski area, where they were shot. The Winniki labor camp continued to exist until the summer of 1943. Then some inmates were sent to a forced labor camp and those who remained in Winniki were shot on July 23, 1943.

The German determination to kill all Jews can be amply demonstrated by the documents below that were issued by the German administration in Eastern Galicia.

The document written in German describes a person named Moses Greif who was born between 1808 and 1812, Jewish religion, district of Janow.

The district governor's office wanted to know the actual birthplace of this person and was searching the record of births of the various communities in the district of Lemberg. The hamlet of Winniki also received a letter of inquiry. The request is dated August 2, 1943, after all the Jews of Winniki had been murdered. We do not know the reason for the search but notice the efficacy of looking for people, especially Jews long after they were murdered. Jews lived in Winniki and probably the mentioned party did so. But there was no definite commitment.

GENERALGOUVERNEMENT
Gouverneur des Distrikts Galizien
Abteilung Innere Verwaltung
Bevölkerungswesen und Fürsorge

Lemberg, den 29.7.1943

An das Kreishauptmann *[illegible]*
in Lemberg
Kr. Lemberg-Land

Betr.: Urkundenbeschaffung
Zeichen: Inn.IV.II./6 u. 770-09/180
(Bei Beantwortung unbedingt anzugeben)

Es wird ersucht, eine wörtliche und beglaubigte Matrikalabschrift der Geburt und Taufe des nachstehenden aufgeführten Kindes zu übersenden

an das   GENERALGOUVERNEMENT
          Der Gouverneur des Distrikts Galizien
          Abteilung Innere Verwaltung
          Bevölkerungswesen und Fürsorge

          L e m b e r g
          Distriktstr.18. Zimmer 115

1. Name des Kindes: *Greif*   6. Tag der Geburt: *1808 - 1812*
2. Vorname: *Moses*   7. Tag der Taufe: ....
3. Name des Vaters: ....   8. Religionsbekenntnis: *israelit.*
4. Beruf des Vaters: ....   9. Geburtsort: *Czernichów*
5. Name der Mutter: ....   10. Gemeinde: *Zagórze*
                                         11. Kreis: *Lemberg-Land*

aus den israelit. Matrikenbüchern von *Rudki*.

Es ist unbedingt eine wortgetreue Abschrift der betreffenden Matrikaleintragungen nebst allen entweigen Vermerken sowie den Angaben über die Eltern auszufertigen. Die Gebühr für die Ausstellung je einer ungekürzten Urkunde beträgt einschl. einer halben Stunde Suchzeit Zl.3.--. Die Stempelgebühr fällt fort, da gemäß Art.160 Z.3 und Art.144 Z.1 des Stempelsteuergesetzes für die von der Urkundenbeschaffungsstelle angeforderten Urkunden keine Stempelmarken erforderlich sind. Wenn länger als eine halbe Stunde nach der Urkunde gesucht werden muß, kann eine Suchgebühr von Zl.1.-- erhoben werden. In diesem Falle ist eine Begründung für die Erhebung der Suchgebühr mitzusenden. Nach Eingang der Urkunde werden die Gebühren einschließl. der verauslagten Postgebühren durch Postanweisung überwiesen. Um beschleunigte Erledigung wird ersucht.

Bemerkung: *Seine Sohn Joachym wurde am 1.5.1847 in Czernichów geboren*

Im Auftrag:
[signature]

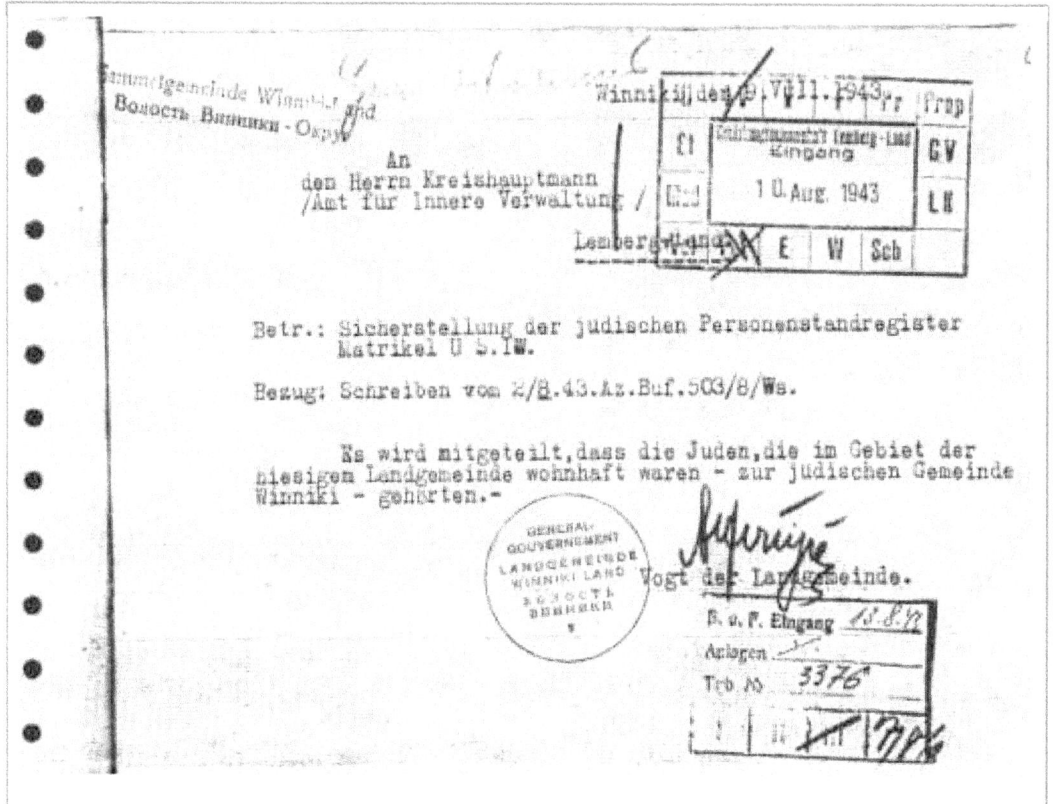

The reply of the Winniki office

Yad Vashem Page of Testimony for Benyamin Mohrer, resident of Winniki, killed in 1942 in the city of Winniki

Yad Vashem Page of Testimony for Rachel Mohrer, née Kenigsberg, resident of Winniki. Killed by the Germans in 1942

Yad Vashem Page of Testimony for Moses Mohrer of Winniki, killed in Belzec

Yad Vashem Page of Testimony

Page of Testimony — 52664

Victim's family name: **LOWENKROWN**
Victim's first name: **HERSH**
Gender: **MALE**

Town of permanent residence: **WINIEK**
Region: **LWOW**
Country: **POLAND**
Number of children: **2**

Circumstances of death: **SHOA**

Submitter:
First name: **XAVIER**
Family name: **MESSALATI**
Street: **YAFO 97/37**
City: **JERUSALEM**
Country: ישראל
Shoah survivor: **No**
Relationship to victim: **RESEARCHER**

Date: 16-05-2010
Place: JERUSALEM
Signature: XAVIER MESSALATI

Yad Vashem Page of Testimony for Hersh Lowenkrown

List of Winniki Jews mentioned in the Yizkor Book of Rabbi Mordechai Gerstel

Family name	First name	Father's name	Mother's name	Gender	Remarks
HOCHBERG	Sheindel			F	
HOCHBERG	Pinie		Sheindel	M	
HOCHBERG	Zelig			M	
HOCHBERG	Esther	Zelig		F	
HOCHBERG	Perl	Zelig		F	
HOCHBERG	Etel	Zelig		F	
MARCH	Wolf			M	
MARCH				F	Spouse:
MOHRER	Benyamin			M	
MOHRER	Ruchel			F	
MOHRER	Reuven		Ruchel	M	
MOHRER	Michal		Ruchel	M	
MOHRER	Shimon			M	
MOHRER	Shmuel			M	
MOHRER	Yossel			M	
MOHRER	Henia	Yossel		F	
MOHRER	Rasha	Yossel		F	
MOHRER	Chaya	Yossel		F	
MOHRER	Dobrish Yossel			F	
MOHRER	Reizel	Yossel		M	
MOHRER	Reuven	Yossel		M	
MOHRER	Zachary			M	
MOHRER	Rivka			M	Spouse: Zachary

Translator's Footnote

1. William Leibner interviewed Karola Lowenkrown–Baum.

CHAPTER V

The Jews of Barszczowice/Borshchovychi

(Borshchovichi, Ukraine)

49°52' / 24°16'

3.8 miles from Nowy Jarczow

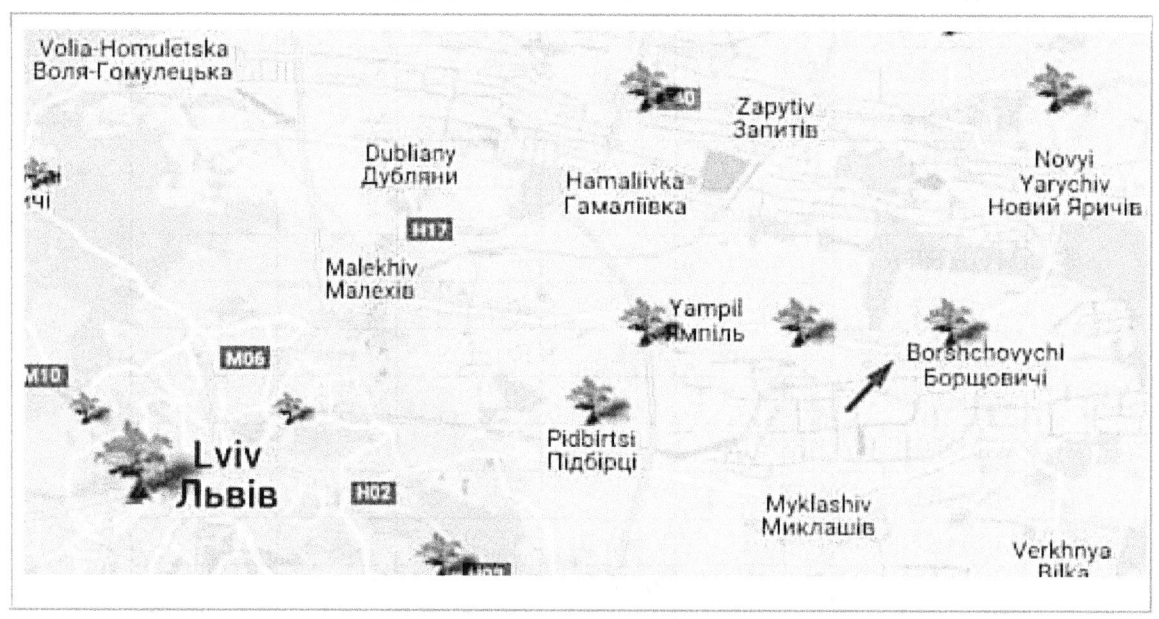

South of the hamlet of Nowy Jarczow on the map is the village of Barszczowice (in Polish, Borshchovychi in Ukrainian). The village is presently in Ukraine

Barszczowice was established in 1574 but its growth was hampered by constant Tartar attacks and invasions. The village was practically erased several times but managed to re–emerge each time. In 1665 the population dropped to merely eight inhabitants. In 1729, the village was acquired by the mighty Potocki family and 20 years later the population consisted of 108 peasants and seven artisans. The village had numerous weaver shops, two distilleries, a brewery and an inn. Following the Partitions of Poland, the village, along with the surrounding region became part of Austro–Hungarian Galicia. The 1820 census lists 127 houses in Barszczowice. Around that time the village was acquired by Jan Maszkowski, a noted Polish painter and tutor of some famous Polish painters.

The arrival of the railway in 1869 boosted the growth of the village, the population of which was predominantly Roman Catholic. According to the 1910 Austro–Hungarian census, the village was inhabited by 2,129 people, including 1,705 Polish speakers, 424 Ukrainian speakers and 79 Jews. Very little is known about the Jewish residents of the village. All of the Jewish religious services were provided by the Jarczow Jewish community. The village continued to expand and reached 2,400 inhabitants in 1928, and was occupied by the Soviets and then by the Germans during World War II. Although far from Ukrainian–populated areas, the village was constantly harassed by Ukrainian underground forces, which resulted in many Polish deaths and a great deal of destruction. With the end of the war, most Polish residents were forced to leave the area and moved to the newly acquired areas of Poland. The village became predominantly Ukrainian. Most of the Jews of the village of Barszczowice were sent to the ghetto of Nowy Jarczow and shared the fate of the Jews of Jarczow.

List of Barszczowice Jews who perished in the Shoa and are mentioned in the Nowy Jarczow Yizkor Book by Rabbi Mordechai Gerstel:

Last name	First name	Father	Gender	Remarks
FLIGELMANN	Hersh Ber		M	
FLIGELMANN			F	Spouse: Hersh Ber
FLIGELMANN		Hersh Ber	M	
FLIGELMANN			F	2 children
KATZ	Hersh		M	
KATZ			F	
KATZ		Hersh	M	
KATZ			F	1 child
KATZ		Hersh	M	
KATZ	Leibish		F	
KATZ	Baruch	Leibish	M	
KATZ			F	Spouse: Baruch and 4 children
KATZ	Menashe		M	
KATZ			F	Spouse: Menashe
KATZ		Menashe	M	
KATZ		Menashe	F	
KATZ			M	
MANTEL	Leibish		M	
MANTEL			F	Spouse: Leibish and 1 child
MANTEL	Hawa		F	
MOHRER	Wowe		M	
MOHRER	Sarah		F	Spouse: Wowe
MOHRER		Wowe	M	Mother: Sarah
WASSNER	Awram		M	
WASSNER			F	Spouse: Awram and family

Kukizow–Kikow–Kyziv
(Kukizov, Ukraine)
49°56' / 24°16'

1.9 miles from Nowy Jarczow

The village of Kukizow is North-west of the hamlet of Nowy Jarczow.

Kukizow was a small village with a small Jewish population, whose religious needs were provided by the Jarczow Jewish community.

Page of Testimony for Awraham Felzner native of Kukiv or Kuziv.
Transported to the death camp of Belzec where he was killed

List of Kukizow Jews who perished in the Shoa and are mentioned in the Nowy Jarczow Yizkor Book by Rabbi Mordechai Gerstel:

Last name	First name	Gender	Spouse
SHTOLTZBERG	Eidil	F	
BERENHOLTZ	Aaron	M	
BERENHOLTZ	Mendil	M	
FELZNER	Hannah	F	Awraham
FELZNER	Awraham	M	
LATT	Baruch	M	
LATT	Meir Leibish	M	
LATT	Mendil	M	
LATT	Yossef	M	
LATT	Freidi	F	
LATT	Sarah	F	
LATT	Tzipi	F	
LATT	Pearl	F	
SAMIT	Haim	M	
SAMIT	Haya	F	
SAMIT	Zlata Riwkah	F	
SAMIT	Yossef	M	
SAMIT	Feitchi	F	
SAMIT	Shmuel	M	

Following is a list of small villages that contained a few Jewish families and some of them are mentioned in the Nowy Jarczow Book.

List of Pekalowice Jews who perished in the Shoa and are mentioned in the Nowy Jarczow Yizkor Book by Rabbi Mordechai Gerstel:

Last name	First name	Father	Gender	Remarks
BLOCK			M	
BLOCK			F	
GOTTLIEB	Daniel		M	
GOTTLIEB			F	
MARGOLES	Shmuel		M	
MARGOLIES		Shmuel	M	
MARGOLIES			F	
MARGOLIES			F	
SCHTAPLER	Pinhas		M	
SCHTAPLER	Shlomo L.	Pinhas	M	nbsp;
SCHTAPLER		Shmuel	F	Spouse: Daniel and 1 child

Podliski Male – Pidlisek
(Podliski, Ukraine)
49°22' / 24°21'

5.9 miles from Nowy Jarczow

List of Podliski Jews who perished in the Shoa and are mentioned in the Nowy Jarczow Yizkor Book by Rabbi Mordechai Gerstel:

Ber, Yaacov – wife, one daughter, one son–in–law

Chiam – from **Podliski**, wife, two children

Henie – her husband **Wolf**, three children, one daughter, one grandchild

Peshe – from **Lissak**, daughter **Ruchtshe**

Shneider, Moshe – wife, four children, one son–in–law

Shpiesback, Beryl – wife **Sarah**, one son

Shtoltzberg, Mordechai – wife, three sons, two daughters

Shtoltzberg, Nissan

Yaacov – his son **Mendel**, his wife **Chava**, two children

Yudele – with his wife

Pobortse – Pidbaritz
(Podbortse, Ukraine)
49°51' / 24°09'

8.1 miles from Nowy Jarczow

List of Pidbaritz Jews who perished in the Shoa and are mentioned in the Nowy Jarczow Yizkor Book by Rabbi Mordechai Gerstel:

Fange, **Zinie** – wife, two children

Fanger, **Nathan** – wife, two children

Mehr, **David** – wife **Tzipe**, three children

Moss, **Israel** – wife, three children

Shaeffer, **Avraham** – wife, four children

Shofer, **David** – wife, three children

Stary Jarczow – Old Jarczow
(Staryy Yarychev, Ukraine)
49°55' / 24°16'

10.1 miles from Nowy Jarczow

List of Stary Jarczow Jews who perished in the Shoa and are mentioned in the Nowy Jarczow Yizkor Book by Rabbi Mordechai Gerstel:

Keller, **Feile** – her brother, his wife, three children

Keller, **Mair** – wife, five children

Kamenopole – Kamenepale
(Kamenopol', Ukraine)
49°52' / 24°10'

6.9 Miles from Nowy Jarczow

List of Kamenopole Jews who perished in the Shoa and are mentioned in the Nowy Jarczow Yizkor Book by Rabbi Mordechai Gerstel:

Hersh – his wife, two daughters, one son–in–law, three children

Milchiker, **Berish** – wife, and daughter

Chapter VI
The Jews of Nowy Jarczow/Novyy Jartchov/Ydalev

(Novyy Yarychiv, Ukraine)

49°52' / 24°16'

3.8 miles from Nowy Jarczow

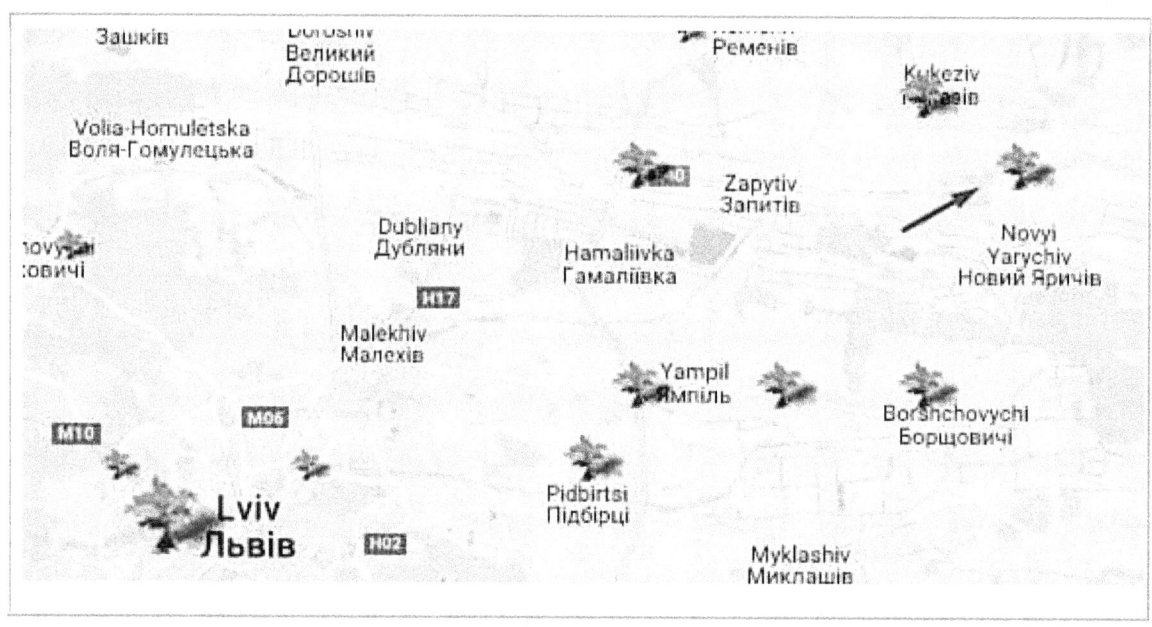

The city of Lwow/Lviv/Lemberg; to the north–east is the hamlet of Nowy Jarczow

Nowy Jarczow was established on feudal lands in about 1451. The town grew and expanded and its status was changed in 1563 to a municipality. The feudal owners of the city permitted the hamlet to grow. Nowy Jarczow faced heavy Tatar attacks in 1578 and in 1695 they almost destroyed the settlement. Slowly the hamlet rebuilt itself and became known as a belt center and a producer of woolen goods.

Jews appeared in Nowy Jarczow about 1577 when it became a town. The Jewish community of 25 people soon disappeared following the Tatar invasion.

A Jewish community appeared again in Nowy Jarczow following the Swedish wars at the beginning of the 18th century. The Jewish settlement grew at the end of the 18th century and in the 19th century. In 1872, there was a big fire that left 2,000 people homeless, mostly Jews. The city slowly rebuilt itself when World War I came along. The Russian forces looted and burned the Jewish homes. Due to the crowded living conditions and poor sanitary facilities, diseases ravaged the Jewish population. On retreating from the city, they burned 200 Jewish homes. People had to live in cellars without heat, and diseases and hunger spread, particularly affecting the Jewish population. Following Russia's withdrawal from the war, the Ukrainians proclaimed a Western Ukrainian Republic that persecuted Jews. The city lost almost 40% of its Jewish population. Many of the Jews left for Lemberg and Vienna and never returned to the city. The city never recovered even after the Polish government restored order in the area.

According to the Polish census of 1921, there were about 986 Jews in Nowy Jarczow and 2,139 non-Jews. The Jews were retailers, peddlers (also supplying agricultural products to the markets of nearby Lemberg) or craftsmen. The Jews were heavily represented in the commercial sector of the city. The Jewish charity fund distributed small loans to craftsmen and merchants. The Jewish community maintained a synagogue, study hall and also several small synagogues or *kloiz* of the various Hassidic sects. The Jewish community also paid the salary of the rabbi. Nowy Jarczow had some famous rabbis, starting with Rabbi David Ashkenazi, the son of the sage Zvi Yoel and the grandson of Rabbi David Katzenelbogen. He was followed by Rabbi Mordechai (died in 1776), Rabbi Arie-Leibush Teomim (died in 1798) and Rabbi Moshe Rapaport (died in 1805). Then Nowy Jarczow accepted its first Hasidic rabbi, Rabbi Shalom Halevi Rosenfeld, also known as the "Rava Prodigy." The local Jewish community was glorified and honored through the services of Rabbi Zeev-Wolf Gerstel who in 1890 became spiritual guide or *More Tzedek* and in 1908 replaced his father, Rabbi Mordechai Gerstel, as the head of the Jewish Judicial Court. Rabbi Zeev-Wolf was famous as a scholar in astronomy. Until his death in 1932, he was considered the premier authority in all of Poland regarding the preparation of the Jewish calendar. The last Nowy Jarczow rabbi was Pesach Zitamor who perished in the Holocaust. In 1933, Rabbi Shmuel Gottesmann–Heller, the Hassidic rabbi or Admor of Laskowicz, established his court at Nowy Jarczow.

The Jews dealt primarily in small trade and crafts, no industry to speak of. There were six Jewish farmers in Nowy Jarczow. The city was poor and offered few opportunities to the younger generation that was desperate to leave.

The Jews of Nowy Jarczow were very pious; most of them were followers of the Belzer Rabbi. The official rabbi of the town was Rabbi Pinhas Zhitomor. He managed to escape to the United States at the beginning of World War II. There there were also a few her rabbis in town. The hamlet also had two burial societies and even had two competing funeral homes

The first Zionist clubs appeared in Nowy Jarczow near the end of the 19th century. The first anniversary of the passing of Benyamin Ze'ev Herzl [Theodor Herzl] was commemorated in the local synagogue with great attendance – a testimony to the increased influence of the Zionists. With the support of the Joint Distribution Committee, a Jewish school was founded in 1922. It had four grades and in its first year it had 80 students (25 boys and 55 girls).

Between World War One and World War II, several Zionist organizations opened local branches: *Akiva* (1932) and its kibbutz preparation corps (1934), the Labor Union of Zion (1934) and a Zionist Youth nest (1933). In the 1928 Jewish community elections the Zionists won five seats, the Hassidic Jews won two seats and the "Nationalists" one seat. In the 1934 municipal elections each of the nationalities – Jews, Ukrainians and Polish – won four seats. The elected Jews were all *Haredi* (ultra–orthodox), due to government influence. In the elections to the Polish Sejm (parliament), 410 Jewish voters (almost all the voters) voted for the Nationalist Party.

Marshal Jozef Pilsudski

There were no social contacts between Jews and non-Jews except for business contacts. Even the school children did not mingle. Moshe Lerner, born in Nowy Jarczow, said he had no Polish friends in the public school and was on occasion beaten up by Catholic children. The only friends he had were the boys from "*cheder*" (religious primary school). In Lerner's testimony at Yad Vashem, he recalled the conversation he had with a neighborly non-Jewish woman: "She told me," Lerner said, "that Marshal Pilsudski died." Marshall Jozef Pilsudski died in 1935. "She told me that my father, Marshal Pilsudski protector of the Polish Jews and other minorities died. And the Jews must go to Palestine. I asked her questions about Palestine and she answered them. According to this woman," Lerner continued, "I did not belong in Poland in spite of centuries of residence in Poland. There was no hate in her words but a mere statement of fact. Of course I knew something about Palestine since I studied in cheder. Her words inscribed themselves in my memory to this day." Polish political parties adopted anti-Jewish slogans and openly incited the local population to hate Jews. Anti-Semitism became an official policy of the Polish government.

This policy eased slightly with the German threats against Poland. Soon Poland was attacked and carved up by Germany and the Soviet Union. Jarczow was in the Soviet sector. The Soviet secret police immediately opened an office in the hamlet and began to arrest well-to-do people and deported them to Siberia, according to Karola Lowenkrown. The Communist Party, which had been banned by Poland, reappeared and took control of the city. Only the Communist press was permitted to exist. Commercial enterprises were nationalized and Jarczow became part of the Soviet economy. Shortages of staples and goods became a common daily event and inevitably a black market developed. The Jewish population was slowly pauperized. Everybody started to work for the government; if you did not work, you were considered an enemy of the nation. The Communist Party interfered with Jewish religious life and limited synagogue attendance.

According to Moshe Lerner, the Soviets came to his father who was a carpenter and told him that the Germans would return to Jarczow and kill all the Jews. The Soviets advised his father and other Jews to move to the Soviet Union where they would be better protected. How the Soviets knew what would happen is a big question; perhaps it was more propaganda than anything else. Lerner's family left Jarczow. "We left Jarczow for the nearby town of Lubicza," Lerner said, "and then headed to the township of Zmerinka that was part of Russia proper. We were not the only Jewish family to have left Jarczow and headed to Russia."

The Germans entered Jarczow during the last days of June or the beginning of July 1941. They immediately arrested 30 Jews and kept them in prison. They were released after paying heavy fines. The Germans began to grab Jews for work. All Jews were ordered to wear an armband with a Star of David on it. Soon a *Judenrat* (Jewish council forcibly organized by the Nazis) was formed that had to provide slave labor to the Germans. The *Judenrat* was headed by Israel Indik. The *Judenrat* also had to provide large gifts to the Germans. All these expenses had to be collected from the Jews and the Jewish police enforced the rules. The Germans and Ukrainians burned the synagogue and the study hall. Toward the end of 1941, the German demand for labor increased daily. Most of the forced laborers were sent to labor camps outside the hamlet, namely to the labor camp of Winniki. These workers were not fed and appealed to the Jarczow *Judenrat* for food.

Jews were forbidden to leave Jarczow and Jews caught outside the hamlet were arrested by the Ukrainian police and often killed. The food shortage became critical in Jarczow. In the summer of 1942, the Germans and Ukrainians rounded up 30–40 old Jews and shot them. Nobody knew the reason. The Germans soon began to move all Jewish people from the surrounding areas to Jarczow. The number of Jews in Jarczow grew and conditions became unbearable, as a shortage of water developed in the ghetto. Epidemics began to appear, including typhus. The Ukrainian city leadership began to worry about the situation and pushed the Germans to take action. Early on January 15, 1943, German and Ukrainian policemen surrounded the ghetto and began to chase all Jews to the market square. The old and the sick were shot on the spot in the market. The rest, about 2,300–2,500 Jews, were led outside the hamlet to prepared ditches. The Jews were forced to cross a bridge over the ditches and while they crossed, the Germans opened machine gun fire. Some Jews were killed while others were wounded but they all fell into the ditches. Nobody survived the action. Many Jews had escaped to the forests, to Polish neighbors or hid in prepared bunkers prior to the final action. The Germans and Ukrainians continued to search the area for Jews and those caught were immediately shot. The Germans kept a small group of young Jews to bury all the dead Jews from the ghetto and from the post-ghetto actions. A small number of Nowy Jarczow Jews survived the Shoah, including Jewish soldiers who were drafted into the Soviet army prior to the German attack on the Soviet Union and some Jews who were deported by the Soviets to Siberia.

Following World War II and the defeat of Germany, Nowy Jarczow was annexed to the Soviet Union. A few surviving Jewish Shoah victims returned to the hamlet and then left. Jews did not want to stay in Nowy Jarczow. They took advantage of the Soviet–Polish agreement that all former Polish residents could leave Nowy Jarczow and settle in Poland. Indeed, most of the Nowy Jarczow Jewish survivors moved to the new areas that Poland received in the West, namely Silesia. The Jews of Nowy Jarczow formed a *landsmanschaft* (home town society) in Wroclaw, Poland and even held a meeting, resulting in a protocol of Jews originally from Jarczow who had survived the war. The list below was produced during the meeting dated November 15, 1946 in Wroclaw, Poland. The list is signed by the regional director dealing with this department. The Jewish member of the Central Committee of Polish Jews, Jonas Torkow also signed the document. There is also a stamp of the AJDC or the American Joint Distribution Committee affixed to the document.

Presently there are no Jews in Nowy Jarczow.

Yad Vashem Page of Testimony for Rasha Mohrer of Jarczow

Yad Vashem Page of Testimony for Shalom Beck of Jarczow

Yad Vashem Page of Testimony for Shmuel Mandel of Jarczow

Wojewódzki Komitet Żydowski
na Dolny-Śląsk
Wrocław, ul. P. Włodkowica 5.
Wydział Ewidencji i Ziomkowstw

Wrocław, 15/XI. 46r.

ZIOMKOWSTWO

S P I S

Żydów, b. mieszkańców miasta J A R C Z Ó W / woj. Lubelskie /
zamieszkałych obecnie na terenie Dolnego-Śląska.

L.p.	Nazwisko i imię	Imiona Rodziców		Rok ur.	Obecny adres	Zawód
1.	Blutman	Salomo	Kopel	1918.	Świdnica	
2.	"	Lea	"	1920.	"	
3.	"	Ssajndla	Icek	1875.	"	
4.	Feuer	Srul		1888.	Wrocław	
5.	"	Adela		1918.	"	
6.	"	Dwojra		1925.	"	
7.	"	Rebeka		1929.	"	
8.	"	Mordko		1930.	"	
9.	Fefer	Halina		1925.		
10.	Fajer	Jakub	Mojżesz	1896.	Świdnica	stolarz
11.	"	Lena	Jakub	1929.	"	
12.	"	Genia	Jakub	1931.	"	
13.	"	Machla	Mordko	1934.	"	
14.	"	Adela	Jakub	1924.	"	
15.	"	Etla	"	1927.	"	
16.	Geistman	Jankiel	Chaim	1888.	"	
17.	"	Jojbe	Jankiel	1935.	"	
18.	"	Rosia	Moszko	1890.	"	
19.	"	Josef	Jankiel	1920.	"	stolarz
20.	"	Ajdla	"	1924.	"	krawczyni
21.	"	Mojżesz	"	1925.	"	blacharz
22.	"	Sara	"	1924.	"	
23.	"	Ruchla	Jankiel	1929.	"	
24.	Kac	Izrael	Baruk	1902.		urzędnik
25.	Lustig	Juda		1918.	Wrocław	rzeźnik
26.	Morenstein	N.		1913.	Nowa-Ruda	
27.	Rundt	Srul	Wikter	1912.	Świdnica	
28.	"	Ssprinca	Srul	1922.	"	
29.	"	Frymet	"	1945.		
30.	Tajg	Leib		1913.	Przemkowo	

Kierownik Wydziału Ewid. i Ziomkowstw
/ Marbach /

Generalny Sekretarz
/ Turkow /

The document is difficult to read so the names are transliterated below.

Last name	First name	Residence	Father	Born	Trade
BLUTMAN	Szlomo	Swidnica	Kepel	1918	
BLUTMAN	Lea	Swidnica	Kepel	1920	
BLUTMAN	Shaindla	Swidnica	Icek	1875	
FEUER	Srul	Wroclaw		1885	
FEUER	Adela	Wroclaw		1918	
FEUER	Dwojra	Wroclaw		1925	
FEUER	Rebeca	Wroclaw		1929	
FEUER	Mordko	Wroclaw		1930	
FEFER	Halina	Wroclaw		1926	
MAJER	Jakob	Swidnica	Mojzesz	1896	Carpenter
MAJER	Lea	Swidnica	Jakob	1929	
MAJER	Genia	Swidnica	Jakob	1932	
MAJER	Machla	Swidnica	Mordke	1934	
MAJER	Adela	Swidnica	Jakob	1924	
MAJER	Etla	Swidnica	Jakob	1927	
GLEISMAN	Jankiel	Swidnica	Chaim	1886	
GLEISMAN	Jejba	Swidnica	Jankiel	1935	
GLEISMAN	Resia	Swidnica	Moshko	1890	
GLEISMAN	Josef	Swidnica	Jankiel	1920	Carpenter
GLEISMAN	Ajdla	Swidnica	Jankiel	1924	Tailor
GLEISMAN	Mojzesz	Swidnica	Jankiel	1925	Metal
GLEISMAN	Sara	Swidnica	Jankiel	1924	
GLEISMAN	Ruchla	Swidnica	Jankiel	1925	
KAC	Israel	Swidnica	Berek	1902	Clerk
LUSTIG	Juda	Wroclaw		1918	slaughterer

NORENSTEIN	N.	Nowa-Rudo		1913	
RUNDT	Srul	Swidnica	Victor	1912	
RUNDT	Szprincz	Swidnica	Srul	1922	
RUNDT	Frymet	Swidnica	Srul	1945	
TAJG	Leib	Przemkowo		1915	

CHAPTER VII

The Khurban Jarczow Yizkor Book

חורבן יארטשוב
ביי לעמבערג

ספר זכרון
לקדושי יארטשוב וסביבותיה

א קורצע באשרייבונג פון ם צוויימען וועלט קריג און פון דעם
יעגעם אן חורבן פון א אידיש שטעטיל אין פוילן, ביז די נעמען פון
די קדושים אלנע זענע היב אפת״צ פארבעו.

בעשריבען
פון
הרב דר. מרדכי גערסטל

ארוי׳סגעגעבען דורך
ר׳ אברהם (אברהמ׳טשע) פוים

Title page of original Yiddish Yizkor Book of Jarczow

A few pages of the original Yiddish text are presented below.

ב"ה   פ א ר ו ו א ר ט

נישטא מעהר דאם אידישע פרומע שטעטיל יארי־
טשוב, אדער ווי אלטע חסידים האבען עס גערופען
"יראה חשובה", דאס ה"סס: א שטעטיל אין וועלכען
עס חאוינען פרומע אידען וואס האבען יראת שמים
און יראת חטא און טוהן חשובה בכל יום וככל עת
וככל שעה וככל רגע. ז" טוהן חשובה יעדען מאג,
יעדע צ"ט, יעדע מינוט, און יעדע רגע.

צוזאמען מים אלע טויזענטער שטעט אין פוילען
רוסלאנד, גאליציען, ליטע און לעטלאנד, איז אויך
י א ר י ט ש ו ב חרב ונחרב געווארען. אין דעם
גרויסען שוידערליכען חורבן פון'ם א"ראפ"אישען
יודענטום בכלל און פון'ם אידענטום אין ד"סמלאנד,
עסמר"ך און פוילען בפרט איז אויך יאריטשוב.

צווישען די 6 מיליאן גרויזאם דערמארדעטע אי-
דען ז"נען אויך דא אונזערע ברידער און שוועסטער
פון י א ר י ט ש ו ב און פון די דערפער ארום
יאריטשוב.

דאס גאנצע ד"מטע פאלק, אלץ ד"טשוקעס, יונג
און אלם, געבילדעטע פראפעסארען און דאקטוירים
צוזאמען מים די א"נפאכע ד"טטע בירגער, ז" אלע
וועלכע האבען מים שטאלץ און מים איבערטריבענער
גאווה און ד"מטער חוצפה זיך גערופען "דאם פאלק
פון דיכטער און דענקער" האבען זיך אין אמת'ן
אבער אויסגעצ"כענט מים מים ז"ערע מעשים אלס "דאס
פאלק פון מערדער און הענקער". ז" די ד"מטע
מערדער, האבען זיך פאראא"ניגט מים די פוילישע
און אוקראא"נישע רשעים מים די זעלבע בלום־
דורשטיק"ים ווי די צעיוכעטע חילדע בעסטיעס. ז"
אלע האבען זיך געהארפען אויף אונזערע אומשול-
דיגע און אומבעוואפענמע ברידער און שוועסטער.
נישט געשאנעמעם ק"ן אלטע און קראנקע, קינדער
און שואנגערע פרויען, אלעסען האבען ז" גרויזאם
געמאמערם און אויסגעהונגערם, אין קאלך אויועגס
פארברענם און אין גאז קאמערען דערשטיקט.

ד"טמע ראקטוירים האבען אפגעשניטען פערש"דע-
נע גלידער פון מענער און ברוטטען פון פרויען
א י ן ז י י ע ר ע פ א ר ב ל ו ט ע ט ן
און מים ד"מטער ט־פליטער פינקטליכק"ם פאמאגרא־
פירט כדי גענוי צו זעהן און צו שטודירען חי
אזוי עם זעהם אויס יציאת נשמה פון א מענש. ז"

האבען מיט דער ד״טשער פינקטליכק״ם גענוי אויס-
גערעכנט װי לאנג עם דויערם ביז א מענש פער-
ברומעם אדער װי לאנב עס דויערט אז א מענש זאל
זיך א בעשטימטען נאז רערשמיקם װערען.ז״ האבען
אויסגעשניטען פון לעבעדיגע אידען די אויגען,
אזוי האבען ז״ אױסגעשניטען די אױגען פון
דעם יאריטשובער רב״ם שװעגערין.- ז״ האבען אנ-
גער״צם אױסגעהוגערטע הינד אויף אידען און
געלאזט פון װילדע הוגגעריגע הינד ז״ לעבעדיגער
ה״ם צער״סען. פון אידישע ר״נע גוםים האבען ז״
געמאכט ז״ה און פון דער הויט פון שעהנע אידישע
קינדער האבען ז״ געמאכט לעמפשע״דס און מאשען
פאר ז״ערע פרױען.

אזוי האבען יענע װילדע אונטערמעפיעס אויס-
געמאמערט,אויסגעהוגגערם און אויך די גרויזאמ-
סטע ארם אומגעבראכם 6 מיליאן אידען אונזערע
ט״ערע ברודער און שװעסטער אױי ז״נען אױך אום-
געקומען אלע אידען פון יאר״שוב און אומגעבונג.
מעהר װי 5000(פינף מויזענד) אידען ז״נען אומגע-
קומען אין יאר״שוב דען אין יאר״שוב איז געװען
א געמא.פון אלע קל״נע שטעמלעך ארום יאר״שוב
און פון אלע דערפער ארום האט מען די אידען פער-
טריבען און נור אין יאר״שוב האם מען ז״ געלאזט,
אבער ז״ האבען געמוזט ז״ן אי״נ״ם יאר״שובער גע-
מא.עס זענען געמען אי״נ״ם געמא אידען פון די
שטעטלעך ארום: פון אלס יאר״שוב,פון קאמינקא
סטראמילאווא,פון גלינע,פון ערעמיסלאן און פון די
דערפער ארום יאר״שוב,פון פודלוסיק,פון ויניע,
זסאלמאניעץ,זארװארזש,יודאלעם,הרעלב,צעפיריח,
קאקיניװ,רידיאנעף,ברסמשימיץ,פון אלע דערפער
ארום יאר״שוב מעהר װי 5 טויזענד אידען זענען
ארס אומגעבראכם געװארען.

צװיטען 1941-1943 אבען אידען געלעבם אין געטא,
אקציע דאס ה״סם די געצליכע גרויזאמע דערמאר-
רונג פון אונזערע ס״ערע ברידער און שװעסטער
אין יאר״שוב איז געטאהן פ׳ און י׳ שבט דעם
ב״נסען און צעהנטען סבם חש״ג פר״מאן ערב סבת ק׳
און סבח ק׳ פ׳ בא.

אין דעם יאהר 1943 דעם 15 און 16 יענער,דא-
מאלס האם אויפגעהערט די קהלה קדושה יאר״שוב צו
עקז״סט״רען.די ד״טשע װילדע ברוינע אונטערבעסטיע

האם צוזאמען מיט פוילישע און אוקראאינישע ווילדע
אנטיסעמיטען אויסגעהארגעט אלע אידן פון יאריטשוב
און פון די דערפער און פון מאנכע שטעטלעך ארום יא-
ריטשוב.

כלם נהרגו ונשחטו נשרפו ונחנקו על קדושת השם
על אלה אני בוכי" עיני" עיני" ירדה מים, הקב"ה ינקם
דמם ישפוך חמתו על האכזרים ועל כל שונאי ישראל
הרשעים וישמידם מתחת שמי ה' ויודע בגוים לעינינו
נקמת דם עבדיך השפוך וירחם על שארית עמו ישראל
ויגאל ישראל בב"א.

אינהאלט

10	יארישוב אויפגעבויט (בבנינה) מעידוש-זייטע
14	יאהרצייט פון די קדושים " "
23	הוטענה פון בארדישעווער צדיק ז"ל "
25	ערב די צווייטע וועלט מלחמה "
28	די צווייטע וועלט מלחמה און דער חורבן "
29	קריעג מיט רוסלאנד "
30	חורבן יארישוב "
43	יזכור "
45	תפלה ליזכור "
48-69	נעמען פון די קדושים פון יארישוב לויט א-ב
70	" " " " ווינים און ידצלוב
72	" " " " בארשטשוויצע
72	" " " " סידליסים
73	" " " " פידבאריץ און קיקיזוב
74	" " " " אלט יארישוב
74	" " " " מעקאלאויטש און קאסטענמאלט
75-78	נעמען פון די לעבענגעבליבענע

תבואה סוחרים,פערד הענדלער און סוחרים פון בהמות
פלאקס סוחרים,לעדער סוחרים און א"נפאכע קרעמער
חעלכע האבען געהאם געהעלבער און קראמען מים פער-
שידענע שמאפם און טוך לי־נחאנר פאר קליידער,פאר
העמדער,זאלאגמעריץ און א"יען געהעלבער,לעדער גע-
העלבער,סענ̈דער,קצבים,גרויסע בעקאנמע גענזהענדלער
וחעלכע האבען נעפיהרם לעבעדיגע גענז קיין לעםבערג
ראדפסניער און צעםפלה̈ענדלער חעלכע האבען געברענגט
םחורה פון לעםבערג,בעלי עגלות חעלכע האבען געפירט
םחורה פון לעםברג און געברענגט סוחרים און געםט
פון לעםבערג און יארםטובער ע"נמאהנער נעפיהרט ק"ן
צארשטםי'היץ,דארם איז געהאן דער באנהוי̈ז(רי סטעי-
שאן) צו פאהרען מים דער באהן קיין לעםבערג אדער אנ-
דערםחאו.אויך פלעגען זיי פיהרען מענשען קי"ן זאדוואר-
ע,דארם איז אויך געהען א באהנםםאנציע(באהנםםעישאן)
בעלי םלאכות זענען געחען אין יארםםוב פערםיע-
דענע:שנ̈דער,שוםמער,םםאליצרם,טעםער(טעפמאכער)בע-
קערם,םלאסערם,םםריקדרייער,מאשען מאכער,עםרה מאכער,
כלי זמרים,מארקזיצערקעם מ̈על־ האבען פערקויפם אין
מארק נעבעקם,צוקערקעם און םפאקלעדם,אויבםם און שאר
ירקות.

אין יארםטוב זענען תמיד געהען בעריהםםע רבנים,
דארם האם געלעבט א גרויםער גאון און צדיק בעקאנט
נוי פים דעם נאםען:דער ראש ישינה.זיין מצבה האבען
די דיםטע רשעים אפילו פים דינאםים נים געקענט צו-
ברעכען.

אין יארםטוב האם אויך נעהאהנם און געלערענט
פאר אונגפעהר 180 יאהר דער גרויםער בעריהםםער
גאון דער בעקאנםער ראועד עילוי הגאון הקדוש ר'
שלום םקאמינקא זצ"ל.פון איהם הארן רעראצעהלם פיעל
קלונגע מעפיוהםיי"ן באבע גי"םל ע"ה האם םיר זעהר פיעל
פון איהם דערצעהלם.מיין באבע ע"ה איז געחען די
אניעםטער פון דעם אלםען יארםםובער רבין חרב הצדיק
ר' שמואל גערםםל זצ"ל די מאכטער פון גאר דעם אל-
טען יארםטובער רבין הרב הצדיק ר' מרדב' גערםטל
זצ"ל דער םסאגער פון רעם גרויםען גאון ר' שלום
םקאמינקא זצ"ל.זי איז געהאן א גרויםע צדיקת און
א גרויםע םלוםדת און האם געקענט דעם גאנצען מנורה
המאור אויפמענדיג.זיא אויך םיין םוטער הצליקה
יענםא גערםםל ע"ה האם מיר דערציילם פון מי"נע
גרויםע זידעם ז"ל און פון אונזערע גרויםע הייליג
פעםערם,פון דעם קאמינקער גאון ר' שלום זצוק"ל און
דעם מאשציםקער צדיק זצוק"ל.אין ראםא רוםקא האט גע-
לעבם א גרויםער עושר,א ר"כער מאלד םוחר,ער האם גע-

THE TRANSLATION OF THE JARCZOW YIZKOR BOOK

A brief description of World War II and the life and death of a Jewish community in Poland with an attached list of authentic names

Described by Rabbi dr. Mordechai Gerstl

Published by Abraham (Abramtche) Boim

New York   1948

THE DESTRUCTION OF JARCZOW

Near Lemberg-Lwow-Lviv

Yizkor Book Dedicated to the Martyred Jews of Jarczow and Nearby Communities

The officers of the Jarczow Relief Society are:

Abraham Baum, Chairman

Kalman {Charlie} Shehr, Treasurer

Rabbi Dr. Mordechai Gerstel

Zeev {William} Taube

Haim Eleazar {Haymi} Sirop

Leizer {Louis} Lacher

Izi Stoltsberg

Abraham Klap

Jacob Zimmerman

Harry Zimmerman

Henry Altman

Ahron Morer

Izi Frostak, Sergeant at Arms

Officers of the Jarczow Society

Zeev {William} Taube, ex-President

Leizer {Louis} Lacher, President

Emanuel Einhorn, Vice-President

Abraham Baum, Recording Secretary and hospital liaison

Izi Stoltsberg, Financial Secretary

Kalman {Charlie} Shehr, Treasurer

Rabbi Dr. Mordechai Gerstel the son of the late Rabbi Meir Gerstel.

Grandson of the late Rabbi Shmuel Gerstl, head of the religious Jewish judicial court of Jarczow.

Abraham nicknamed Abramtche Boim donates his free time and his energies to the Jarczow relief society and to the many people in need. He devotes himself to the new arrivals that need all the help they can get. We have to thank him for his devotion to the relief job. He also saw to it that the Jarczow Yizkor be printed and helped to erect a monument to the martyred Jews of Jarczow.

All his work is done with devotion and sincerity.

FOREWARD

Jarczow, the saintly pious little town no longer exists.

A town whose pious Jews constantly repented, each hour, each instant. They repented all of the time, minute-by-minute and second- by- second.

Yaritchiv like other Jewish towns in Poland, Russia, Galicia, Lithuania, and Latvia were destroyed in the tragic destruction of European Jewry. Amongst the 6 million murdered Jews, we also find our brothers and sisters from Jarczow and all of the surrounding areas.

The entire German nation, young and old, professors, doctors and simple Germans prided themselves as the nation of poets and thinkers. In reality, however, they distinguished themselves as the nation of murderers.

They joined hands with Polish and Ukrainian murderers and attacked our defenseless brothers and sisters. They did not spare the old, the sick, the children or the pregnant women. They tortured, starved, burned and gassed the Jews.

German doctors severed limbs from living Jews and led them bleed to death. The pain and agony of the dying was recorded with great precision. They calculated the length of time needed to die or to asphyxiate the Jew. They removed the eyes of Jews, as was done to the daughter-in-law of the Rabbi of Jarczow. They incited their hungry dogs to attack Jews. The Germans converted Jewish bodies into soap and the skins of Jewish infants were transformed into lampshades or pocket books.

Thus, did the wild beasts exhaust, torture and kill 6 million Jews. Dear brothers and sisters, amongst them were the Jews of Jarczow and the nearby areas. More than 5000 Jews were killed in Jarczow for the town had a Ghetto and all the Jews in the area had to move into it. No Jew was permitted to live outside the Ghetto. It contained Jews from the following hamlets: Old Jarczow v, Kamionka, Stromilowa, Gline, and Premishlan. All the Jews from the following villages were forced to move to the Ghetto: Podlusik, Winiek-

Zoltaniec, Zadworsche, Idalev, Hereniv, Tzefiriv, Kokiziv Ridianeff and Borshtziviec. Of course the Jews of Y Jarczow itself were also moved to the Ghetto.

The Jews lived in the Ghetto from 1941-1943. Then the final actions took place on the 15th and 16th of January 1943, the ninth and tenth day of the month of Shvat, Tashag, Friday and Saturday when the torah portion of " Ba " is read. With these actions, the Jewish communities ceased to exist. The area became free of Jews.

I am shedding tears for all those martyred people that were slaughtered and killed. I hope G-d will avenge the blood that was shed. And destroy the perpetrators of these evil deeds and extend his divine protection over the remnants of the people of Israel and lead them to Salvation.

Galicia Yizkor Book

Table of Contents

The list refers to the Yizkor Book

P.10 Jarczow and its buildings

P.14 Memorial Day or Yahrzeit

P.23 Hoshana of the Berditchever Rabbi

P.25 Eve of World War II

P.28 World War II and the Destruction

P.29 War with Russia

P.30 Destruction of Jarczow

P.43 Yizkor

P.45 Prayers before Yizkor

P.48 Names of victims of Jarczow

P.70 Names of victims of Winiek and Ydalev

P.72 Names of victims of Borshtzewice

P.72 Names of victims of Podlusik

P.73 Names of victims of Fidbaritz and Kikizov

P.74 Names of victims of Alt Jarczow

P.74 Names of victims of Pekalowitch and Kamenfale

P.76 Names of survivors

Jarczow is located in Eastern Galicia near Lemberg, close to Premishlan, Bobrika, Kamionka, Stromilowa, Zolkwa, Mikolayev and Gline.

The Jewish population consisted of about 600 families prior to World War I. There was a slight decline after war.

When I speak of Jarczow, of course refer to the area of the market surrounded by Jewish homes that formed entire streets. Here were located the Jewish store keepers with their long beards and side curls, wearing large black velvet hats and long black coats, selling their wares. In the side streets, the Jewish women were busy cooking, baking, cleaning and sewing as befitted Jewish daughters. The scents of Jewish cooking permutated the air of the streets. Happy and sad Jewish tunes emerged from the open windows of the workshops where Jewish tailors, shoe makes, seamstresses and spinners were working. From other places, the chant of the torah study prevailed, especially the chant invoked in the study of the Talmud.

I am shedding tears for all those martyred people that were slaughtered and killed. I hope G-d will avenge the blood that was shed. And destroy the perpetrators of these evil deeds and extend his divine protection over the remnants of the people of Israel and lead them to Salvation.

The big beautiful synagogue, the big study center, the house of the late rabbi Samuel Gerstel, the house of the young rabbi Zeev Wolf Gerstel, the synagogue of the Belzer Hassidim, the synagogue of the late Rabbi Alter Eichstein, the Kaminker shul, the many torah study centers where Jewish children studied Torah, the study room of Horev, the religious girls school of the Agudat Israel, the Hebrew day school, the slaughter house, the kosher butcher stores, the public bath house, the Mizrahi association, the Zionist association, the Bikur Holim society {to visit sick people}, the Lina society {to provide sleeping accommodation for needy people },the mutual aid society} and the road leading to the forest or forests where the youth promenaded on Saturday afternoon and inhaled the fresh country air while admiring G-d's world.

As in other Polish cities, the Jews of Jarczow engaged in trade and conducted business. There were forest merchants, wood merchants, grain merchants, horse and cattle dealers, flax and leather merchants, grocery and storeowners who sold all kinds of goods. Material for coats and dresses, ribbons and threads for sewing, metal and leather stores, inns and slaughter houses, geese dealers led their flock to Lemberg, farmers and delivery men brought their goods from Lemberg, carriages transported goods and people to Lemberg, Jarczow residents headed for Borshewic or Zadworshe to take the train to Lemberg or further. Jarczow did not have access to the Railroad

There were many artisans in Jarczow, tailors, shoemakers, carpenters, rope makers, pot makers, bakers, locksmiths, pocket book makers, talit makers, embroidery makers, musicians and vendors that sold sweets, cookies, chocolates, fruits and vegetables in the market. The city was always known as the residence of famous scholars, the most famous, was the Rabbi known as the head of the Yeshiva, the Germans were unable to blast his tombstone.

180 years ago, lived and studied in Jarczow, the famous Raver

scholar, known as the late Rabbi Shlomo Kaminker. Many wise stories and tales are related to him, as told to me, by my grand mother, Gittel. She was the sister of Rabbi Samuel Gerster, the daughter of Rabbi Mordechai Gerstl who was the son-in-law of the Kaminker Rabbi. She was a pious and well read woman. My late mother, Yente Gerstl, told me the stories of my grand parents and uncles, notably the story of the Kaminker Rabbi and later the Mozitzer Rabbi.

In the city of Rawa Russka, there lived a very rich person; he was a forest merchant. He lived in a big house with many rooms, expensive carpets covered the floors, he was called the Count and behaved like one.

He had many servants and each day rode in his coach riven by two horses. The family had no children. One Yom Kippur eve, when all the worshippers left the study Chader after the services, he began to implore the Almighty to grant him children, he cried, begged and recited the Psalms all night long and finally exhausted, fell asleep. Suddenly, an old man appeared in his dream and told him that he was destined to continue this manner of life but his lamentations had the desired effect. In his sleep he consented to the change and shortly thereafter his business declined rapidly. His wife gave birth to a son who will become the well-known Kaminker Rabbi and a daughter who will be my great-grandmother.

The brother-in-law of the Kaminker Rabbi was my great-grandfather, Rabbi Mordechai Gerstel, the very old Rabbi of Jarczow. His father was Rabbi Samuel Gerstel.

The Rabbi, Mordechai Gerstl had a sister, she was a very pious woman. Most of her grand children managed to escape the clutches of the Nazis. They are all in Brooklyn. Rabbi Dr. Moshe Blech, his brother, Rabbi Ben Zion Blech, and the youngest brother, Rabbi Tzvi Blech. The oldest grand son has already children who are Rabbis and a daughter who is a professor at Columbia University.

After the demise of Rabbi Mordechai Gerstl, his son, Samuel Gerstel became the Rabbi of Jarczow. He was nicknamed the old Rabbi. His son, Rabbi Zeev Wolf Gerstel was called the young Rabbi of Jarczow. He was also a scholar in Botany and Astronomy in spite of his Hassidic appearance, he wore white pants and socks in the tradition of Hassidic Rabbis.

The Rabbi Samuel Gerstel also had four daughters: Beile Gerstl, Blima Blick, Sarah Rivka Katz and Sheva Gottesman, the wife of the late Rabbi Betzalel Gottesman. Following World War I, Rabbi Zeev Wolf Gerstl moved to Lemberg and the Rabbi of Jarczow became his brother-in-law, also the son-in-law of the old Rabbi of Yaritchiv, Rabbi Betzalel Gottesman. Mr. Abraham Baum and the Jarczow society brought the Rabbi to the USA where he remained for several years. They supported him and hoped that he will remain in the country But he refused to bring his family to the USA and returned to Jarczow, where he died shortly thereafter.

His son, Rabbi Haim Gottesman assumed the position of Rabbi of Jarczow. For almost two hundred years, the Gerstel family provided Rabbis to the town. The last Rabbi, a grandson of the old Rabbi, led about 2000 Jews to the cemetery where he recited with confessions and with the "Shema" on their lips they were shot on the 9th and 10th day of the month of Shvat, Tashag {1943 }.

G-D WILL AVENGE THE BLOOD THAT WAS SHED

In Jarczow there were many religious teachers and two ritual slaughterers. Reb Hershali, the teacher dressed up and entertained the people on Simhat Torah and they enjoyed his frolics. Another teacher, Reb Alter Shamesh also thought children and he was called Reb Mr. Alter or Reb master teacher. There were also Talmudic teachers: Itchele {Itche }Sanes, Tzadok Melamed, Reb Israel Avishes, Reb Nissan Melamed and a cantor named Reb Yokali for Jews liked to hear their prayers.

The extent of religious piety and Hassidic life can best be described by the fact that the mailman of Jarczow, an employee of the Austrian Imperial Postal System, had along beard and side curls and wore a *shtreimel* {special fur hat worn by Hassidim} on Saturday just like the other Hassidic Jews. His name was Yaacov Baum, his son Avraham Baum cane to the USA and was very involved in the Jarczow society. He helped publish this memorial book.

Mr. Avraham Baum tried very hard to bring me over to the USA. With the assistance of Max Reiser from Baltimore I was finally brought from Vienna to the USA before the Nazis closed the gates.

Jarczow had a few Jewish representatives that spoke on behalf of their Community with the central authorities. These representatives were all deeply religious Jews and sat on the committees with their non-Jewish representatives.

Prior to World War I, the Mayor of Jarczow was my uncle, Itzhak {Itche] Blick, the old Rabbi's son-in-law, he was a scholar and a pious Jew. He managed quite well the city and installed lights in the market which lit the entire city of Jarczow. Jarczow also had a large society of "Bikur Cholim " whose members visited the sick and helped with their basic needs. There was also a

"Lina "Society whose members would sleep in the house of the sick and help them if they were alone. All of these good deeds were performed as good deeds or mitzvoth. Jarczow had a mutual aid society that extended interest free loans and enabled repayment over long periods of time so as to enable the needy to survive the bad times. Former Jarczow residents supported this fund and thus helped their brothers and sisters in the old country.

Mr. Abraham Baum and the relief society of Jarczow received many thank you letters and notes from people that borrowed from the fund. They also received many thank you letters from the torah study center "Horev " and the religious girls school of the Agudat Israel for their financial support.

Each year, on Lag Ba'omer {thirty-three days in the Omer}, the study cycle of the Talmud finished. Scholars with large foreheads and sharp eyes assembled on that day in the synagogue to hear the final lines of their study program. Where-upon, a big celebration was held with speeches, lectures and Hassidic tunes. Yaritchiv also had a large Zionist association. The younger members studied Hebrew following World War I. They prepared themselves to immigrate to Palestine. Many of the younger Jews also left for the USA where they managed to establish themselves.

As in other Polish cities, there was no lack of poor Jews. Jews gave charity to help the poor ones to survive until market day. Every Wednesday was market day and the poor Jews would congregate in the market and beg charity. Some of these were invited to the homes for the Saturday meals. Every poor Jew was assigned to a home so that he would have a meal. Those that didn't have a place, went to the house of the old Rabbi. Very often there were a few guests at my grand father's table, the more the merrier. These people were not called beggars or schnorrers but Sabbath guests.

Every Wednesday was market day and several times a year there big fairs which attracted Ukrainian and Polish farmers that came to town to buy goods: leather, metal pots, axes, pails, plows, nails, materials for shirts, dresses and ribbons. The farmers sold: cows, bulls, horses, chickens, wood, all kinds of grain, vegetables, potatoes and various fruits.

Jews bought and sold and earned their livelihood from the market and the fairs. Late in the day, especially summer days, when the farmers left town and the dust from their carriages settled down. One could see Jews with long black beards and side curls, dressed in long kaftans or overcoats with their large black velvet hats rushing to the Synagogue, study center or small place of worship.

Young boys with their velvet Kippot and side curls, adorable little Moshes, Shlomos, and Avrahams with beautiful big eyes following their mothers or grand fathers who headed to the synagogue to offers thanks to the Almighty and to ask Him for health, income, deliverance and the reconstruction of Jerusalem.

Women sat on the porches or on wooden benches in front of their homes or stores and inhaled the fresh air that blowing from the forest while exchanging stories about good deeds performed by Rabbis. They also exchanged some local gossip about families with problems, bright children in town, girls about to be engaged which will be followed by weddings, children that did not excel in their studies, erc... Young beautiful maidens walked quietly and took in the scene, lowered their eyes when they met fellows, still glances were exchanged and eyes continued to follow each other. Some times, greetings were even exchanged.

In the study centers sat young scholars, as described by Haim Nachman

Bialik {Hebrew and Yiddish poet}, and studied while chanting the particular tune used in the study of the Talmud. So said Rabba...

Others read secretly the Hebrew papers " Hatzfira" and " Hamatzpe". The students, pale and dreamy eyed, faced big Talmud books and tried to answer difficult questions posed by the Rambam {Rabbi Maimonides}.

All this stopped with the arrival of the Sabbath or a holiday. The town assumed a complete different atmosphere. All the stores were closed and from all the windows there were lights, the reflections of candlelights, in short lights everywhere.

Jews with patriarchal faces dressed in black satin kaftans wearing shtreimels {fur hats} on their heads, rushed to the synagogue. Children with velvet caps or hats, dressed in their best Saturday clothing, their peyot {side curls} curled, cluthing in their hands their sidurim {prayer books} went to the Synagogue to greet the Sabbath Queen {allusion to Saturday}. Here they sung " Lecha Dodi " {prayer dedicated to the arrival of the Sabbath}.

All this changed with the arrival of the High Holidays. Entire families from the nearby villages came to spend the Holiday in town. Jews greeted each other with the famous blessing: A Healthy New Year.

The fear of Yom Kippur was on everybody's mind, Jews began to forgive each other and desisted from expressing sharp opinions or strong personal feelings, each person rushed to the synagogue to pray and beg for the fulfillment of his wishes.

Who can forget Kol Nidrei Night in Yaritchiv? The synagogue was packed with people dressed in "kittels" {white robes}, white kippot on their heads, wrapped in their big talitot. The place was lit by hundreds of candles that reflected the saintly faces of the Jews. Amongst them was my grandfather dressed in white, the kittel and the big talit with the big ornamental fringe. He cried on the way to the synagogue and then preached to the congregants while holding the scroll in his hands. Finally, he shouted the line that begins the Kol Nidrei service: Or Zaruah...All the congregants shed tears, especially the women's section.

Jews prayed to the Almighty for forgiveness, life, income, spiritual up lifting, good influence on the children, good marriages and the speedy arrival of the Messiah. Jews could be happy without theaters or movies, which didn't exist in Yaritchiv. They enjoyed the Cantor, Yokel, who chanted their prayers, or the young Rabbi who blessed the lunar month or the singing on the way to the "Tashlich " {casting the sins upon the water} service. The young married scholars supported by their families continued their studies of the Jewish past, the difficult questions that arose in the study of the " Halacha " {Jewish religious legal codex}. These men escorted the Rabbi when he entered the

Grevlie Street that led to the river where the Rabbi cast his sins while the entourage sang and were merry.

Amongst, the students that studied at the Jarczow Synagogue, will be the future Chief Rabbi of Lemberg, Rabbi Dr. Shmuel Gottesman. He will tell me later, I was in your grandfather's study center and studied under him.

Another famous student studied there, my cousin, Moshe Gerstl. He was a grand son of the old Rabbi, the son of Mordechai Gerstel. He became a famous Architect in Haifa, Israel. He designed the shopping center of the Hadar Carmel neighborhood in Haifa, which was the nicest shopping center in the Middle East.

The joy of the Jew was at its height when he participated with the Rabbi in the dancing of the " Simhat Torah " Holiday. The teacher Hersali entertained the congregants who were a bit high since they already had a few drinks and tasted some of the baked items. This holiday marked the end of the Holiday season and the Jews felt comfortable with all the mitzvoth that they had performed during the month of Tishri. So many mitzvoth were performed: the blowing of the shofar, the fasting and asking for forgiveness on Yom Kippur, the sitting in the Sukkah, the blessing of the lulav and finally the reading of the last section of the Torah.

The Jews were overjoyed with Simhat Torah and they expressed it by dancing and singing, especially Hassidim. The festivities reached a high point at the Synagogue of Rabbi Alter Eichenstein.

Some of the grand children of Rabbi Abele, brother of the old Rabbi of Yaritchiv, managed to survive and live in New York. They are: Rabbi Dr. Moshe Blech and his brother. A grand son of the Rabbi Alter Eichenstein also survived and resides in New York. His name is Rabbi Elimelech Horowitz.

Jews offered thanks and praise to the Almighty and Creator of the Universe. They sang the famous Hassidic song, " Haaderet Vehaemunah " {praising the faith}, to whom? To whom? To the Eternal One. The understanding and the blessing to whom, to whom? to the Eternal One.

Every Saturday afternoon, at the "Shalosh Sudah Meal " {third meal of the day held in the synagogue or in the study center}, the Jew sat and listened to spiritual matters which uplifted him. He sang praises to the Lord and escorted the Sabbath out with song and joy while partaking in drinks and snacks. With the exit of the Sabbath, the Jew went home and lit a special candle and sat down to a small meal which consisted of borsht and potatoes or herring and vodka. He was happy and joyful with the departure of the Sabbath and it gave him fortitude to withstand all the pressures that the Polish anti-Semites created to deprive him of his livelihood as by the great increase of taxes. The Sabbath songs strengthen the Jew to face the daily problems and to look forward to a better world.

"Siman tov and mazal tov, yehei lanu u lekol Israel, amen" {We and all of Israel should have a good omen and good luck, amen, loosely translated}, *"David Melech Israel Hai vekayam..."* {King David of Israel is alive and well. reference to the Jewish people}, "G-d said to Jacob fear no one but me", songs about the good old prophet Eliyahu who took a poor Hassid and made him into a rich person in one night. The pauper became a wealthy man that devoted himself to serve G-d without the need to worry about the daily necessities. The good old prophet and the Messiah of the house of David will soon lead us to our salvation. Eliyahu, please come and bring with you the messiah so that we can be redeemed. {these were the type of Sabbath songs}

Throughout the year, when an engagement, wedding, circumcision or party celebrating the first-born took place, the Jew of the Polish Shtetl really celebrated. The "huppa" or canopied ceremony took place in front of the Synagogue at night, the bride and the groom were escorted from their respective homes by crowds of people who danced, sang and made merry. The people lit candles and placed them in the windows. The throng of spectators carried candles, the jesters told their lines, the musicians reinforced by well-known bands from Premishlan played music. The youngsters were happy and the less religious crowd participated by singing the songs such as the "huppa" by Meir Hartner.

Standing there before the synagogue a group is performing good deeds so many boys and girls carrying on, laughing and mingling. Suddenly, voices urging silence, silence. Suddenly, voices urging silence, things are moving sha sha.

Forward musicians of the first order Fiddler Moshe Rimfel, Haim Yekil on the Cello, Beryl with the Cymbals, Snat Avramel with the Drum, Yona with the Tambourines, Walt Tremeiter give a honk The music is moving through the streets Tam Tram Tram Tam Tam... Ta Ta Ta.

{This is a loose translation}

Religious Jews partook in the wedding by dancing the " Mitzvah Dance". The dancer and the bride hold a handkerchief while dancing so as not to touch each other. The crowd danced, sang and chanted popular songs and special religious songs such as: the first preference, the first preference have Jews because...

Who was to know that all these happy Jews would be killed solely because they were Jews.

Fifty years ago, some Jews in Jarczow saw little hope and decided to leave for America. Later they brought their relatives to this Country. Soon they created a Jarczow Young Men Association to help the new immigrants from their town, to provide assistance to the relatives who wanted to come and to help the relatives in Jarczow.

Jarczow became poorer as a result of World War I. Polish and German anti-Semitism raised a generation of Jew haters, the university students, the officials and the farmers began to discriminate against the Jews.

The latter was beaten in the streets and his beard fequently shaved. Jewish stores were boycotted etc. The story of Pszytic {a modern pogrom} repeated itself in many places.

The Jew haters, the followers of General Haller manhandled Jew on the trains and in public places and prevented people from buying in Jewish stores. Many public buildings and places had big signs saying:" Hit the Jew". The Polish, Ukrainian and Rumanian Jew haters cooperated with their

German counter parts. They tried to imitate the German Nazis and published all the hate in the local press.

The Poles wanted to ban the ritual slaughter of animals to prevent the Jews from eating meat. It took a great deal of efforts to postpone the implementation of the law. They wanted to destroy the Jew and divide his goods. The Germans and Poles only thought of ways to kill the Jew and deprive him of his goods.

Young Jews began to emigrate, some went to the USA and some organized themselves in Zionist organizations with the aim of leaving for Palestine. Even the religious youth organized itself in the ranges of " Mizrahi Hatzair " or " Hashomer Hadati "and the very religious " Agudat Israel "

Had a youth group ready to go to Palestine. Unfortunately, a small fraction, a very small fraction managed to Leave Poland. The entire Polish Jewry, the bulk of the Jewish population remained in Poland.

In the big and little cities, Jews continued to live as though nothing happened. The Jewish politicians did not see the German danger. They did not foresee the forging of a unification of German nationalism and Polish anti-Semitism aimed at the Jew. The air was being polluted with anti Jewish poison. The Jewish Politicians lulled themselves into a false sense of security and hoped that things will blow over.

EVE OF WORLD WAR II

When the Austrian sadistic room painter became German chancellor in 1933 and became the leader of a nation of murderers and executioners, the situation of the German Jewish Community became very precarious.

The Germans issued decrees, the "Nuremberg Laws" Aimed at the Jews. Thousands were sent to the various Concentrations Camps, many were deprived of the property and still many left Germany as fast as they could.

The Germans constantly wrote in newspapers and in books that they will destroy the Jews. Their speeches stated that they will kill all the Jews, erase every trace of Jewish life, and convert Germany into a "Judenrein " nation.

This aim will also be exported to the world. They said that Harman {the Purim story} tried to kill the Jews but we will finish the job. This aim was constantly repeated in the German press. The youth and the university students constantly paraded in the streets and sung songs stating the day will come when Jewish blood will drip from their knives and this will cause great joy in the heart of the German nation.

The Germans planned not only to rob the property of the Jews but the "lower-beasts"{I call the Germans lower beasts since I don't want to insult the four legged beasts that attack only when hungry} also planned to rob Jews everywhere of their goods.

Every day thousands of Germans paraded and sang songs stating that we will march in rows and everything will tremble; today Germany belongs to us and tomorrow the world.

Frequently I run from the streets of Vienna in 1938 and sought refuge when I heard the parade approaching and the songs about the dripping Jewish blood and world domination.

The big nations such as England, France and the smaller nations read the German press and Hitler's book " Mein Kampf '. Their representatives in Germany reported to them the German scene. All the Nations thought that Germany was only interested in the Jews and their property. Maximum, they were interested in granting Germany a piece of Czechoslovakia, the Sudaten region. If however Germany was interested in war, it could mean one thing, an attack on Russia. This did not bother most of the nations. They were rather pleased with the job that the Germans were doing to the Jews and some even hoped that the Germans would carry out their preaching. The Poles began a vicious attack against the Jews that resulted in Jews being beaten in the streets of Poland. We Jews warned the big nations that the Germans were not only interested in killing Jews but aimed at war.

In the summer of 1936, the League of Nations met in Geneva, Switzerland. A German Jewish refugee, Mr. Lukas, committed suicide in the big convention hall. All the papers reported the event and knew the reason for the act of desperation. He saw that nobody tried to stop Hitler, on the contrary, everybody sacrificed the Jews and let him do whatever he wanted.

Mr. Lukas was buried in a small cemetery and the Jewish correspondent, A. Halpern, writing for the " American " wrote a column entitled " Grave number 236 " in which he describes the Rabbi's eulogy. The Rabbi said: You journalists can stop these outrages, you have the means to reach public opinion, what are you waiting for, but the world was not disturbed.

I personally wrote to a German newspaper and called the attention of the politicians to an important book that was published by an important Austrian Jewish official, Yona Krepel {later shot}. The book entitled the "12th hour "described the forthcoming dangers and I pointed them out but I was ignored.

AUSTRIA

The ninth day of Adar, Friday to Saturday, March 12th 1938, Germany occupied Austria and now the Austrian Jews were in deep trouble. Thousands of them were sent to prison and Concentration camps, thousands died and still thousands fled. The Austrian Jewish exile began then the Czechoslovakian exile.

A year later, 1939, the Jews of this country faced the same problem. The brown German beast drank Jewish blood but they realized that the supply is limited. For 80 million Germans the spoils were limited. They smelled blood and wanted more and more, more killing and robbing. They attacked Poland and the greatest tragedy begun.

WORLD WAR II AND THE DESTRUCTION OF POLISH JEWRY

The first of September 1939, Friday, 17 days in the month of Elul, Tarzat {5699}, thousands of German planes flew over the Polish Country side and dropped thousands of bombs on Polish cities. The bombs spread terror and death amongst the population and clouds of fire rained down on Poland. Thousands of Jewish Polish soldiers lost their lives on the battlefields and thousands were killed by the bombs. Thus World War II begun.

In three weeks, the Germans occupied Poland and destroyed hundreds of Jewish communities, hundreds of thousands of Jews were killed or sent to the Concentrations camps, and Ghettos were created in the bigger cities where thousands died of hunger and disease.

Thousands of Jews ran to East Galicia {part of Poland not occupied by the Germans} with empty hands, they ran on foot through forests and plains until they reached Lemberg and Yaritchiv. Thousands of Jews came from very distant little towns to this area.

According to a secret agreement signed between Germany and Russia, Lemberg was to be occupied by the Russian forces on September 17, 1939, Yartchiv was also included in this zone. Life became very difficult. Russia began to prepare for war and took away many Jews. Inflation was rampant, so food items became very expensive. The Jews accepted the difficulties thinking that the worst was over; they were saved from German occupation. Thus they hoped for the best. But this illusion was soon destroyed.

WAR WITH RUSSIA

Twenty-seven days in the month of Sivan, Tasha {5701}, Friday, the 22nd of June 1941, the Germans started the war with Russia. The German army entered Russia and occupied the Polish cities, they soon reached the city of Lemberg. The city fell on the 29th of June 1941, or the third day of the month of Tammuz, Tasha. The city of Yaritchiv and the surrounding area also fell on the same day. Thus began the destruction of Jewish Lemberg and all the other Polish and Russian cities, amongst them also Jarczow.

The Jews of the Jarczow ghetto lived in a living hell. The Germans shot, hacked and knifed to death Jews. When the Germans entered the city in 1941, they detained the following Jews:

1. Avraham Indik, 2. Itzhak Lewenberg, 3. Yossef [Yoshe] Kreiner, 4. Itzhak Weissman, 5. Israel Binstein 6. Abele Hochberg, 7. Yossef {Yoshe} Shorr, 8. David Peah, 9. Israel from Podlisk {Feivel's son}, 10. A Jew from Vienna, and 3 recent arrivals.

They were taken to Remaniv where they joined another party of 30 Jewish men, women and children. All of them were now driven to a big farm in Remaniv. Here some were thrown into the waste pit while others were hacked to death and then thrown into the waste pit which was eventually covered with sand and all the injured Jews were asphyxiated.

Later, they started to burn the Synagogue and the study center of Yaritchiv. A Ukrainian brought a drum of gasoline and spread the liquid over the holy places. The flames devoured the Synagogue and the study center. These holy places where Jews prayed and implored their G-d daily went up in smoke.

A few days later, the Ukrainians discovered that the ornaments of the torah scrolls were hidden in the home of Reb Alter, the Melamed, the teacher. They went to his house and took a silver torah crown and put it on his head. Another crown was put on the head of a Jew of Radinetz. They were forced to march through the streets of Yaritchiv singing and dancing. Eventually their beards were torn from their faces and they died as a result of the wounds that they sustained.

Shortly thereafter, the Germans rounded up 100 Jews for work and send them to a labor camp. Reuven Fehler describes this camp in his letter. He worked on the streets of Lemberg leading to Yaritchiv and then to Brody. The name of the German organization was Todt. He received 70 grams of bread a day and a half a liter of water. The SS and the Ukrainians beat them daily. Many Jews died or were killed in this camp. This was the situation of the camp in 1941.

Passover 1942, a few Jews met in Yaacov Druker's home to pray. They began the first day holiday service whereupon two SS men and some Ukrainians burst into the place and found Itzhak Baum, the talit ornamental maker, reading the Torah. They ordered him to remain standing while they burned his beard. Their fury increased when he did not utter a sound. The other Jews in the room were beaten and some even murdered. Few Jews made it out alive.

In the holiday of Shavuot, 1942, the Judenrat of the Jarczow received an order to send all the elderly Jews out of the Ghetto. They will be sent to be burned. The first to be sent was Shragai Feivel Blick with his Talit and phylacteries. The second was Beile Yente Blick, related to the Firs, 3.Yaacov Hitz, 4. Hersh Kimmel and his wife, their sons and wife's, 5.Idel Lewenberg and his daughter, 6.Rachel Shpatz and her daughter, 7. Ethel Karfil, 8.Golda Haitches, 9.Avraham Weissman, 10.Yente Fleher, 11. Zalman, the non-talker, shoemaker, 12. Avraham Hersh Shteiner. These and many more were taken in the direction of Lemberg and burnt alive somewhere along the road.

Then the murderers decided to tackle the old cemetery of Jarczow.

The Jews were forced to uproot the tombstones and pave the streets with them. All the tombstones were uprooted except the one for the head of the Yeshiva. This tombstone remained erect in spite of the attempt to blast it with dynamite. The stone was finally hoisted from the ground and placed on the bridge of the village of Baninen.

Yeshai {Yeshayahu} Ber Klihiner was kicked to death by a German. He started kicking him in the stomach and did not stop until he was death.

The ninth day of the month of Shvat was very cold and frosty. The Germans decided to drive the Jews out of the ghetto. About 2500 Jewish men, women and children were driven to the forest. Some managed to hide in special hiding places but most were driven out of their places. The Germans and the Ukrainians searched every place. Sick people and small infants were driven out into the bitter cold. The day was Friday, 9 AM. About 2500 Jews started to march to the forest. Along the road they were split into two groups. One group continued to march to the forest while the other group was led to the cemetery.

Many sick people and children died during the forced march while others were shot, stabbed or knifed to death. The white snow became tinted with blood.

The road to the forest where young Jews used to promenade and hum tunes was the scene of the mass murder. Here were hacked to death many men, women and children. Among them: Moshe Ger, Meir, Shmuel, Wolf the glazier, Mendel Kahane etc.

Blood and more blood was everywhere. Pure innocent blood of small children, Moshelech, Schlomelech, Saralech, Rivekalech etc.. The desperate cries for help were heart braking but to no avail. All the Jews in the forest were shot.

Missing paragraph. Please insert it after the line dealing with the death of Ber Klihiner and prior to the paragraph of the ninth of Shvat. On the ninth day of Shvat, the 15th of January, 1943, Doctor Melnik of Podlisk, may his name be erased, and the German murderer Shtarnebel, Mayor of Yartchiv, may his name also be erased forever, gave the order to kill the Jews of the ghetto.

A NAZI PLAYS WITH LIVING EYES

The second group was heading to the cemetery. At the head of the column was Rabbi Haim Gottesman, his wife, all his children and his entire family. Followed by Hersh Tzigler with his children, Yossef {Yoshe} Ber Schwartz with his wife and children, Meir Asterman with his wife and children and the other two thousand Jews of the ghetto. The crying and yelling of the children and the weeping of the mothers was heart braking. Suddenly, a German murderer noticed the attractive daughter-in-law of the Rabbi as she was staring with her sad eyes. He approached her and removed her eyes with a knife. She fell to the ground, blood poured over the snow. The German played with her eyes.

The Rabbi began to recite out loud the last prayer for the living. The last prayer recited by the last Rabbi whose grandfathers led the Jewish community for over 200 years. The entire Jewish community repeated the last prayer and they shouted the Shema Israel when the German began to shoot them. They died with the Shema on their lips.

Later the murderers began to search the hiding places of the Jews in the Ghetto and in the forests. All the Jews that were discovered were tortured and then shot. Only a few young people managed to escape and survive among them Reuven Feler who described everything that took place in the community. His testimony and the one by Rabbi Katz were the basis for this book.

The murderers caught Moshe Yaacov {Yankl} Meizel and his wife, their daughters with their husbands. They fired several bullets at Moshe Yaacov but no bullet hit him. An SS man took his pistol and fired point blank at Moshe Yaacov who fell saying the Shema.

The mother of Reuven Feler, Keile Feler and her son-in-law Shiya Mimelman and his children were hung. The mass execution took two days, the ninth and the tenth day in the month of Shvat. On the sixteenth day of Shvat, the Germans broke into a hiding place, which contained Haim Ker, Mendel Kimmel, Moshe Yaacov {Yakel} Kerner, and some wives and children. There were 33 people in the hiding place. A Ukrainian revealed to the Germans the hiding place. All the Jews were shot at the cemetery.

Nine weeks later another hiding place was discovered. Hidden were Mrs. Kimmel and her children. The mother and her daughters were shot and the son managed to escape and survive the war.

When the Russian front neared Jarczow, the Germans did not want the Russians to see so many dead people in the forest and at the cemetery. They ordered the local authorities to assemble the bones and limbs that were scattered over the area to one area and burned them.

There are no more Jews in Jarczow. There is no sign that a Jewish community existed in this town. Everything is destroyed, even the cemetery, was destroyed. Every tombstone was uprooted.

The murderers destroyed everything in Jarczow.

We bemoan the fate of our brothers and sisters in Jarczow and the 6 million saints that were murdered. For those we shed our tears.

With the first publication of the news of the destruction of European Jewry, many groups organized themselves in New York to help the remnants of that community. The Young Men's Relief Society of Jarczow also organized a special relief society which consisted of:

Abraham Baum, chairmnan

Rabbi Dr. Mordechai Gerstel

Zeev Wolf {William } Taube

Kalman {Charlie} Shehr, treasurer

Haim Eleazar {Haymi} Sirop

Leizer {Louis} Lacher

Izi Stoltsberg

Abraham Klap

Jacob Zimmerman

Harry Zimmerman

Henry Altman

Ahron Morer

The object of the relief committee was to help the survivors of the " Shoah", the erection of a monument for the martyrs who were so brutally killed and not even buried, and to publish a Yizkor book which will describe the Jewish community of Jarczow so that future generations will have a record of what transpired and how the community ended up.

The book will also contain the names of the Jewish martyrs and will serve as a living remainder for the Jews that were never properly buried.

For two thousand years the Jews moved from place to place, never accepted, always despised and persecuted, beaten and exiled. No day passed without some threat or problem, no hour without evil things in the making and no minute without some plague.

But what occurred in our times never happened since creation and was never done to a nation.

The German murderers killed about 6 million Jews, a third of the Jewish people. Presently, even the bitter Diasporah is over, there is no more Jewish life in Poland.

All enemies of the Jewish people created Libels directed at the Jews. From Apian in Egypt, down to the ritual murders and the Protocols of Zion, in modern times. All of these accusations are in the spirit of Balak, curse the Jews. But Balak also gives advice to the Jews, they should assimilate, visit entertainment places with beautiful women, they should be invited to the homes of their neighbors and most important, they should mingle with the surrounding population in order to become part of the total population. We must remember all our enemies.

We can't accept the premise that once we behave like other people we will be totally integrated. Remember Israel, this is a very serious commitment, and assimilation will not eliminate the hatred.

The prophet Jeremiah laments: "Your tragedy {Jewish} is as vast as the sea and who will heal it..."Rabbi Yaacov Itzhak Rheines comments that it is difficult to heal the Jewish tragedy which is similar to a sea disaster. When a city is destroyed or devastated by an earthquake, the signs remain for a long period of time. However at sea, no trace remains of a disaster. Within minutes everything disappears. Unfortunately, great tragedies that afflicted the Jewish people are soon forgotten. This is the reason that we must record the events that took place in our lifetime so that a recorded living memorial exists for eternity.

Unfortunately, this small Yizkor book, similar to other Yizkor books or journals, serve as living testimony to future generations. We must draw the bitter inferences of the exile, what nations can do to other nations and how low nations can sink spiritually.

Israel must remember the martyrs, the Jewish nation must remember the slaughter of the 6 million Jews, our brothers and sisters, murdered so tragically. The Jews must remember the bitterness of the exile; each Jew must remember the meaning of the exile, the meaning of statelessness or the lack of government. Unfortunately, we Jews tend to forget easily the problems of the exile. Already in the desert of Sinai, we forgot the problems that we faced when we were slaves in Egypt and kept talking about the good old days we had there. The fact that they drowned Jewish children was not remembered.

The holy Torah tells us, remember what Amalek did to you. Many mitzvoth and other good deeds are based on the basis of our exit from Egypt. In relation to this event, the Torah says remember the days between the generation allusion to the need of repeating the exit from Egypt in each generation. The prophet Mika also begs us to remember what the king of Moab urged Belem to do and what the latter answered:

"What I did from Shitim to Gilgal was to protect the Israelites in their struggle for survival"

We must remember all our enemies. Amalek, and his great son Hamman. They wanted to kill all the Jews. The second enemy, Balak, says: 'go and curse this nation {the Jews}". Jew haters always schemed or accused Jews of doing evil things to their neighbors in order to enrage them into action against the Jew.

While we sat in exile we thought that we have another Jerusalem and this is the cause of our sin. Thus writes the famous Yaacov Amdin in his introduction to the prayer book of Rabbi Javitz. We thought that we had another Jerusalem while living in exile and this is the cause of all evils that afflict thy Jewish people. Furthermore, listen to me brothers and sisters who reside in exile, remember G-d and the holy city of Jerusalem. Try not to make plans to remain in foreign countries since an attachment develops and it weakens the desire to return to the homeland. This was the sin of ancestors who refused to return to Israel and caused great pain and suffering to generations of Jewish people...

In Spain, Jews lived a beautiful and prosperous life as they did in other countries and then they barely escaped with their lives.

Our sages say that G-d said to Itzhak: "If the Jewish people had earned the merit, the Torah would have started with the letter T {Taff} but it did not start". Apparently, the Jewish people did not have the needed merit, for even after the expulsion of Spain they did not go to Palestine where they could have started to rebuilt the country and Jewish moguls like Baron Rotshield or Gootman or Magnats of the caliber of Brodsky or Wissotsky could have helped financially the country so that with the proclamation of the Balfur Declaration there would have been a large Jewish population. The population might have grown to about 3 million Jews, but this was not to be.

Still we implore the Almighty to protect us from all the evil schemers and He should have mercy on His people.

Let Israel remember the exile. Remember what the Amaleks and the Jew haters did to the Jews. Write it down in the Torah said G-d to Moses, according to the sages, for unrecorded events disappear in history.

Let Israel remembers the heroes of the land of Israel. Let the people remember the heroes that sacrificed themselves for the Jewish nation, for a free Jewish land in Israel. We all have to remember to assist in every possible manner the struggle for a Jewish homeland based on the principles of the torah.

THE SECOND YIZKOR

Let Edom and Ishmael remember the second Yizkor. They and all the other Jew haters should remember from the pages of history that nations that start with the Jewish people pay the consequences.

We Jews believe in the sanctity of the torah and the prophets. As the Prophet Jeremiah says: "Israel is holy to G-d and all detractors will pay for their deeds". Let all the Jew haters remember that those who intend to inflict harm or pain to our people will be punished by G-d. The Germans are already beginning to pay for their deeds and more is in store for them and their deeds.

Let Edom, Ishmael and other Jew haters stop their plans to harm the Jewish people. Let them permit the establishment of a Jewish state and let them leave the Jews in all the countries to live their full life in Peace.

PRAYER PRIOR TO THE YIZKOR FOR THE MARTYRS

Remember G-d the 6 million saintly souls of the martyrs of Jarczow and the surrounding communities. Names that we inscribed and those who were omitted for lack of knowledge.

Remember G-d the souls of the 6 million Jews, remember the names of our brothers and sisters. They were so brutally murdered for the sole reason that they were Jews. Our sages tell us in the Talmud that: "when Jerusalem was captured, 400 Jewish boys and girls were seized and taken aboard ship to be sold as prostitutes. When the destination became known to the children, one of the girls asked whether they will enter Paradise if they jumped ship, one of the older boys quoted a line from the psalms to the effect that G-d saves all souls, from the depth of the sea to the mouth of the beast". All the children jumped ship with the "Shema "on their lips and drowned.

Thus G-D accepted the souls of the martyrs with love and understanding. All the souls that the wicked people threw to the wild beasts or starving dogs that ripped the bodies apart and they were never buried, the souls of the burned on the heaps or ovens, the souls of the asphyxiated in the gas chambers, the souls of those bodies that lost limbs and the souls of those that were never properly buried in accordance with the Jewish law.

These souls join the souls of those that were killed for 2000 years because they were Jews. The souls of the Jews of Yartchiv and surrounding areas that were inscribed and those that were omitted for lack of knowledge and those of the 6 million, please, merciful G-d remember them all as pure saints and add them to these that have long passed away in our long history of the exile. The souls of the 6 million martyrs that were killed, butchered, burned, asphyxiated and exterminated in the final solution for the sole reason of being Jewish, sons of Abraham, Itzhak and Yaacov.

Merciful Father, please find them a permanent resting place in your realm and with the resurrection join them with the other parts of Israel. Amen.

There before your throne, let all the souls intervene on behalf of the survivors in order to strengthen them in rebuilding their shattered Jewish life and home as well as enable all of us to help build the holy land. And the Rock of Israel will help free the people of Israel and will send us a special messenger who will deliver the people of Israel and the Kingdom of Israel will arise again. The third day of the week, the Torah reading section of Pinhas, twenty days in the month of Tammuz. Quote:" No religious community shall remain without the Shepard". Tashah {1948}

Rabbi Dr. Mordecai Gerstel, son of Rabbi Meir Gerstl, grandson of Rabbi Shmuel Gerstel of Jarczow.

The author writes the story with tears in his eyes and hopes for salvation.

Rabbi Mordecai Gerstl, 2376 Ryer Avenue, Bronx 57, NY

SPECIAL PRAYER FOR THE MARTYRS

Master of the world and all the souls, you remember the history of creation and command all earthly creatures; there are no mysteries for you since creation.

You remember all the persecutions and tortures that were imposed on us throughout the years of bitter exile in all countries and places. You see all the sites where they slaughtered thousands of men, women and children. You saw all the piles of burning bodies that were our brothers and sisters. You saw these events since our exile from our homeland. They all died with the "Shema" on their lips.

You remember the 6 million Jews that were killed, slaughtered, burned and asphyxiated. You saw how the German murderers and their local helpers savagely attacked your people. They killed, devoured and spilled blood as though it was water. They fed the birds of prey and the wild beasts, your followers. Thousands of Jews were thrown to the hungry dogs, which tore them apart while still alive. Their souls left them while their bodies were being devoured. There are no secrets before you.

You know the entire plan how the German murderers skinned young Jewish men and women and converted the skins into objects.

You know how the filthy cruel Germans tore the limbs of fathers, sons, wives and daughters until they died and their pure souls left them. You wrote in your holy torah as written by Moses, your servant:" that no Ox and its offspring can be killed on the same day". Yet, thousands of fathers were killed before their sons. Daughters and sons were killed before their mothers. Thousands of Jews were burned alive and from some of the bodies they extracted the fat to convert it to soap in order to wash away their blood stained hands. Please remember all these deeds since you remember everything.

Heavenly father, who resides in His distant realm. Please care gently for the saintly communities that sacrificed themselves for You, and the saintly souls that were killed, butchered, slaughtered and burned since we left the homeland, and all the souls of the 6 million Jews who were the sons of Abraham, Itzhak and Yaacov, killed slaughtered, burned, asphyxiated, and wiped out by a hail of bullets. And the souls of the just and the pious that are close to you. Remember them and all the other saints who sacrificed themselves for you. Avenge the innocent blood that was spilled and direct your anger at the murderers and their helpers who ignored your divine protection of the Jewish people. Judge and punish them for the evil things that they did to your people.

May it be thy will Lord our G-d to have pity on us, and the people of Israel. Assemble all the dispersed and direct our hearts and minds to serve You and the creatures of the universe, to love the people who perform good deeds, give us the strength and cure us of the ills of the exile, and help us for Your sake.

Bless all the soldiers that are guarding day and night the holy country against the enemies. Please have mercy, assemble the rejected ones, lead us to the holy land, and help us build the country and the temple in Jerusalem. There we will study the Torah, the good deeds of loving and helping people, the ways of bringing people and nations together.

And Oh Lord grant therefore glory to Thy people, bring joy to the land, gladness to the country and all the wicked people should vanish like smoke in the air, and remove the evil dominion from the face of the earth. No nation shall fight nation. Grant peace and well being bless and bestow loving kindness and mercy unto us, and all the Nations that respect and defend us. Cast a Peace Net upon us, and all the nations of the world. And you alone will lord over Mount Zion, the dwelling place of Thy glory, and Jerusalem, Thy holy city as it is written in the Holy Scriptures: " The Lord shall reign forever, Thy G-d, Oh Zion, shall be sovereign unto all nations. And the Lord will rule over the land and that day G-d will be One and His name Unique. Amen

And those are the names of Jewish people in the city of Jarczow and the surrounding areas that were killed, slaughtered, burned and asphyxiated on the ninth day of Shvat, reading section in the torah, "Ba "and on the holy Shabbat, the tenth of Shvat, Tashag {1943}

When G-d will order the resurrection, He will instruct the appropriate angel to account for all the pious, the just and the converts that died in His name.

CHAPTER VIII

LIST OF JEWISH VICTIMES MEMORIALISED IN THE JARCZOW YIZKOR BOOK

LIST OF TRANSLITERATED YIDDISH NAMES TO LATIN LETTERS

And those are the names of Jewish people in the city of Jarczow and the surrounding areas that were killed, slaughtered, burned and asphyxiated on the ninth day of Shvat, reading section in the torah, "Ba "and on the holy Shabbat, the tenth of Shvat, Tashag 1943.

When G-d will order the resurrection, He will instruct the appropriate angel to account for all the pious, the just and the converts that died in His name.

Jews of Jarczow prior and and during World War II

Compiled by William Leibner

KEY
JAR-Jarczow
Resi-live
G-Gender
SO- Source
YB-Izkor Book
D-Disposition
S-Shoah

LAST NAME	First Name	Resid	Father	Mother	G	Spouse	Child	SO	D
AARON	Miriam	JAR	Aaron		F			YB	S
AARON	Raphael	JAR	Aaron		M			YB	S
AARON	Rachel	JAR	Aaron		F			YB	S
ACKSTEIN	Zalman	JAR			M			YB	S
ADLER	Reuven	JAR			M			YB	S
ADLER	wife	JAR			F	Reuven		YB	S
AFTEWITZER	Riwkah	JAR			F			YB	S
AFTEWITZER	Haya She	JAR			F			YB	S
AFTEWITZER	Malka Bre	JAR			F			YB	S
AKSELRAD	Pessah	JAR			M			YB	S
AKSELRAD	Feige	JAR			F	Pessah	+	YB	S
AKSELRAD	son	JAR	Pessah	Feige	M			YB	S
ALTMANN	Yekil	JAR			M			YB	S

ALTMANN	wife	JAR			F	Yekil		YB	S
ALTMANN	daughter	JAR	Yekil	wife	F			YB	S
ALTMANN	3 sons	JAR	Yekil	wife	M		+fam	YB	S
ANDEK	Bunem	JAR			M			YB	S
ANDEK	wife	JAR			F	Bunem	+child	YB	S
ARLENDER	Dudel	JAR			M			YB	S
ARLENDER		JAR			F	Dudel		YB	S
ARLENDER	Zalmen	JAR			M			YB	S
ARLENDER	Esther	JAR			F	Zalmen	+ 7 child	YB	S
ARLENDER	Israel	JAR			M			YB	S
ARLENDER	Riwtche	JAR			F	Israel	+ 2 child	YB	S
ARLENDER	Itzhak	JAR			M			YB	S
ARLENDER	Tzipi	JAR			F	Itzhak	+ 2 child	YB	S
ARLENDER	Yossef	JAR			M			YB	S
ARLENDER	wife	JAR			F	Yossef	+ 2 child	YB	S
ARLENDER	Husband	JAR			M			YB	S
ARLENDER	Hannah	JAR			F	Husband	+ child	YB	S
ASHKENAZI	Moshe	JAR			M			YB	S
ASHKENAZI	wife	JAR			F	Moshe	+ child	YB	S
ASTERMAN	Itche	JAR			M			YB	S
ASTERMAN	wife	JAR			F	Itche	+ 2 child	YB	S
ASTERMAN	Uri	JAR			M			YB	S
ASTERMAN	wife	JAR			F	Uri	+ child	YB	S
ASTERMAN	Meir	JAR			M			YB	S
ASTERMAN	wife	JAR	Meir	wife	F	Meir		YB	S
ASTERMAN	daughter	JAR	Meir	wife	F			YB	S
ASTERMAN	Meir	JAR			M			YB	S
ASTERMAN	Blime	JAR			F	Meir		YB	S
ASTERMAN	husband	JAR			M			YB	S
ASTERMAN	Ratzi	JAR			F	husband		YB	S
ASTERMAN	Simha	JAR			M			YB	S
ASTERMAN	wife	JAR			F	Simha		YB	S
ASTERMAN	Bernard	JAR			M			YB	S
ASTMAN	Hinde	JAR			F			YB	S
ASTMAN	Motel	JAR		Hinde	M			YB	S
ASTMAN	Shmuel	JAR		Hinde	M			YB	S
ASTMAN	Henia	JAR		Hinde	F			YB	S
ASTMAN	Ethel	JAR		Hinde	F		+ husban	YB	S

AUSTEIN	Itzik	JAR			M			YB	S
AUSTEIN	Esther	JAR			F	Itzik	+ 6 child	YB	S
AUSTEIN	Beile	JAR			F			YB	S
AWRAHAM		JAR			F		+ child	YB	S
BACH	Haim	JAR			M			YB	S
BACH	Rachel	JAR			F	Haim	+ child	YB	S
BALTEN	Itzhak	JAR			M			YB	S
BALTEN	Moshe	JAR			M			YB	S
BALTEN	Esther	JAR			F	Moshe	+ 6 child	YB	S
BARER	Moshe	JAR			M			YB	S
BARER	wife	JAR			F	Moshe	+ child	YB	S
BARER	Haim	JAR			M			YB	S
BARER	Sarah	JAR	Haim		F	husband		YB	S
BARER	husband	JAR			M			YB	S
BARER	Haim	JAR			M			YB	S
BARER	Hila	JAR			F	Haim		YB	S
BARER	Michael	JAR			M		+ fam	YB	S
BARITZ	Haim Wol	JAR			M			YB	S
BARITZ	Golde	JAR			F	Haim W	+ fam	YB	S
BARITZ	Yehezkel	JAR			M			YB	S
BARITZ	wife	JAR			F	Yehezkel		YB	S
BARITZ	Israel	JAR			M			YB	S
BARITZ	Toibe	JAR			F	Israel		YB	S
BARITZ	Lemil	JAR			M		fam	YB	S
BARITZ	Mindel	JAR			F	husband		YB	S
BARITZ	husband	JAR			M			YB	S
BARITZ	son	JAR	husband	Mindel	M			YB	S
BARITZ	daughter	JAR	husband	Mindel	F			YB	S
BARITZ	Pithiya	JAR			M			YB	S
BARITZ	wife	JAR			F	Pithiya		YB	S
BARITZ	daughter	JAR	Pithiya	wife	F			YB	S
BARITZ	Wite	JAR			F		+ child	YB	S
BARTER	Itche's	JAR			F			YB	S
BAUM	Yaakow	JAR			M			YB	S
BAUM	Awraham	JAR	Yaakow		M			YB	S
BAUM	Itzhak	JAR			M			YB	S
BAUM	wife	JAR			F	Itzhak	+ child	YB	S
BAUM	Wolf	JAR			M			YB	S

BAUM	wife	JAR		F	Wolf	+ 3 child	YB	S
BAUM	Karolina	JAR		F	M		YB	S
BAUM	Riwkah	JAR		F			YB	S
BAUM	daughter	JAR	Riwkah	F			YB	S
BAUMAN	Hersh	JAR		M			YB	S
BAUMAN	wife	JAR		F	Hersh	+ fam	YB	S
BAUMAN	Henoch	JAR		M			YB	S
BAUMAN	wife	JAR		F	Henoch	+ fam	YB	S
BAUMAN	Walke	JAR		F			YB	S
BECK	Yente	JAR		F			YB	S
BECK	daughter	JAR	Yente	F		+ fam	YB	S
BECK	Benyamin	JAR		M			YB	S
BECK	Meite	JAR		F	Benyami	+ 4 child	YB	S
BECK	Haim	JAR		M			YB	S
BECK	wife	JAR		F	Haim	+ 4 child	YB	S
BECK	Shalom	JAR		M			YB	S
BECK	Esther	JAR		F	Shalom	+ fam	YB	S
BECK	Asher	JAR		M			YB	S
BECK	Tzirel	JAR		F	Asher	4 child	YB	S
BEER	Dawid	JAR		M			YB	S
BEER	wife	JAR		F	Dawid	+ 2 child	YB	S
BEINHOLTZ	Sarah	JAR		F			YB	S
BELLER	husband	JAR		M			YB	S
BELLER	Yuta	JAR		F	husband	+ 4 chil	YB	S
BERENSTEIN	Hersh	JAR		M			YB	S
BERENSTEIN	wife	JAR		F	Hersh	+ fam	YB	S
BERENSTEIN	Hershel	JAR		M			YB	S
BERENSTEIN	wife	JAR		F	Hershel	+ child	YB	S
BERGER	Husband	JAR		M			YB	S
BERGER	Hawa	JAR		F	Husband	+ child	YB	S
BETIG	Yossel	JAR		M			YB	S
BETIG	Miriam	JAR		F	Yossel	+ 6 child	YB	S
BIENSTOCK	Israel	JAR		M			YB	S
BIENSTOCK	wife	JAR		F	Israel	+ 2 daug	YB	S
BILLER	Itzhak	JAR		M			YB	S
BILLER	Helen	JAR		F	Itzhak		YB	S
BILLER	Mordecha	JAR		F		+ fam	YB	S
BILLER	Mintche	JAR		F			YB	S

Surname	Given	Town	Father	Mother	Sex	Spouse	Other	Src1	Src2
BILLER	Mordecha	JAR			F			YB	S
BILLER	Ruchtche	JAR			F		+ child	YB	S
BILLER	Awraham	JAR			M			YB	S
BILLER	wife	JAR			F	Awraham	+ child	YB	S
BILLER	Elikum	JAR			M		+ child	YB	S
BILLER		JAR			F			YB	S
BILLER	Shifra	JAR			F			YB	S
BILLER	Mintche	JAR		Shifra	F			YB	S
BILLER	Elsa	JAR			F			YB	S
BLANKHAMMER	Aaron	JAR			M			YB	S
BLANKHAMMER	Brontche	JAR			F	Aaron	+ fam	YB	S
BLAUSTEIN	Haim	JAR			M			YB	S
BLAUSTEIN	Henie	JAR			F	Haim	+ 4 child	YB	S
BLAUSTEIN	Yossef	JAR			M			YB	S
BLAUSTEIN	Eva	JAR			F	Yossef	+ fam	YB	S
BLAUSTEIN	son	JAR	Yossef	Eva	M			YB	S
BLAUSTEIN	Israel	JAR			M			YB	S
BLAUSTEIN	wife	JAR			F	Israel		YB	S
BLAUSTEIN	son	JAR	Israel	wife	M			YB	S
BLAUSTEIN	wife	JAR			F	son	+ 2 child	YB	S
BLAUSTEIN	Yaakow	JAR			M			YB	S
BLAUSTEIN	wife	JAR			F	Yaakow	+ 2 child	YB	S
BLAUSTEIN	Zalmen	JAR			M			YB	S
BLAUSTEIN	Sarah	JAR			F	Zalmen		YB	S
BLAUSTEIN	Mordecha	JAR	Zalmen	Sarah	M			YB	S
BLAUSTEIN	Sarah	JAR			M	husband		YB	S
BLAUSTEIN	husband	JAR			M			YB	S
BLAUSTEIN	Nichte Ha	JAR			F			YB	S
BLICK	Malka	JAR			F			YB	S
BLICK		JAR		Malka	M			YB	S
BLICK	wife	JAR			F	Mordechai		YB	S
BLICK	Blime	JAR	Rabbi		F			YB	S
BLICK	Baruch	JAR			M			YB	S
BLICK	wife	JAR			F	Baruch	+ child	YB	S
BLICK	Hersh	JAR			M			YB	S
BLICK	wife	JAR			F	Hersh	+ 2 child	YB	S
BLICK	Baruch	JAR			M			YB	S
BLICK	wife	JAR			F	Baruch	+ child	YB	S

Surname	Given Name	Town	Father	Mother	Sex	Spouse	Other	Source
BLICK		JAR			F			YB S
BLICK	Idis	JAR		Hannah	F		+ 3 child	YB S
BLICK	Mordecha	JAR			M			YB S
BLICK	wife	JAR			F	Mordechai		YB S
BLICK	Feiwel	JAR			M			YB S
BLICK	daughter	JAR	Feiwel		F			YB S
BLICK	Shmuel	JAR			M			YB S
BLICK	Dworah	JAR			F			YB S
BLICK	Shmuel	JAR			M			YB S
BLICK	wife	JAR			F	Shmuel		YB S
BLICK	Shmuel	JAR			M			YB S
BLICK	Deworah	JAR			F			YB S
BLUTREICH	Leib	JAR			M			YB S
BRATTER	Yossef	JAR			M		+ fam	YB S
BRATTER	Mendel	JAR			M	and fam		YB S
BRATTER	Meir	JAR			M		+ child	YB S
BRATTER	Meir	JAR			M		+ child	YB S
BRATTER	Itche	JAR			M		+ fam	YB S
BRATTER	Awraham	JAR			M			YB S
BRATTER	Mali	JAR			F	Awraha	+ 3 child	YB S
BRATTER	Hersh	JAR			M			YB S
BRATTER	wife	JAR			F	Hersh		YB S
BRATTER	Malka	JAR			F		+ fam	YB S
BRATTER	Freide	JAR			F		+ fam	YB S
BRATTER	Klaman	JAR			M		+ fam	YB S
BRATTER	Shlomo	JAR			M			YB S
BRATTER	Ethel	JAR			F	Shlomo		YB S
BRATTER	daughter	JAR	Shlomo	Ethel	F			YB S
BRATTER	Sarah	JAR	of Shlomo		F	husband		YB S
BRATTER	husband	JAR			M			YB S
BRATTER	Ber	JAR			M		+ child	YB S
CIFFER	Naphtali	JAR			M			YB S
CIFFER	Rishe	JAR			F	Naphtali		YB S
CIFFER	Haya	JAR	Naphtali	Rishe	F			YB S
CISTERNER	Yaakow	JAR			M			YB S
CISTERNER	Eti	JAR	Yaakow		F			YB S
CISTERNER	Malka	JAR	Yaakow		F			YB S
DAWID		JAR			M			YB S

Surname	Given Name	Town	Father	Mother	Sex	Spouse	Other	Source
DAWID		JAR	DAWID		F			YB S
DENIWER	Nachman	JAR			M			YB S
DERNIWER	Shmuel	JAR			M			YB S
DERNIWER	wife	JAR			F	Shmuel	+ sons	YB S
DIENGOTT	Regina	JAR			F			YB S
DIWALD	Hersh	JAR			M			YB S
DIWALD	Yaakow	JAR			M			YB S
DIWALD	Nehema	JAR			F			YB S
DIWALD	Yaakow	JAR			M			YB S
DIWALD	Hersh	JAR			M			YB S
DIWALD	Hasia	JAR			F			YB S
DONNER	Gdalia	JAR			M			YB S
DONNER	Tzivia	JAR			F	Gdalia	+ 6 child	YB S
DONNER	Yoshe	JAR			M			YB S
DONNER	Esther	JAR			F	Yoshe	+ 2 child	YB S
DORF	Yaakow	JAR			M			YB S
DREIFUSS	Aaron	JAR			M			YB S
DREIFUSS	Sarah	JAR			F	Aaron		YB S
DREIFUSS	daughter	JAR	Aaron	Sarah	F			YB S
DRUCKER	Drucker	JAR			M			YB S
DUDIE		JAR			M			YB S
DUDIE	wife	JAR			F	DUDIE	+ 3 child	YB S
ECKHAUS	Zintche	JAR			F	Artche	+ child	YB S
ECKHAUS	Pearl	JAR			M			YB S
ECKHAUS	Sheindel	JAR			F	Zintche	+ child	YB S
ECKHAUS	Uri	JAR			F			YB S
EHRENWERRT	Motel	JAR			M			YB S
EHRENWERRT	wife	JAR			F	Motel		YB S
EHRENWERRT	Artche	JAR			M			YB S
EHRENWERT	Dawid	JAR	Bunem	wife	M			YB S
EHRENWERT	wife	JAR			M			YB S
EHRENWERT	Artche	JAR			F	Dawid	+ 2 child	YB S
EHRENWERT	wife	JAR			M			YB S
EICHENSTEIN	Chaim Mo	JAR			M			YB S
EICHENSTEIN	Deworah	JAR			F	Haim Mordechai		YB S
EICHENSTEIN	Eides	JAR	Haim Mo	Deworah	F			YB S
EINHORN	Emanuel	JAR			M			YB S
EISENSHER	Eliezer	JAR			M			YB S

Surname	Given	Town	Father	Mother	Sex	Spouse	Other	Src	
EISENSHER	Brontche	JAR			F	Eliezer	+ 2 child	YB	S
EISENSHER	Yaakow	JAR			M			YB	S
EISENSHER	Rachel	JAR			F	Yaakow	+ 2 child	YB	S
EPSTEIN	Alter	JAR			F			YB	S
EPSTEIN	Pearl	JAR			M			YB	S
EPSTEIN	Bunem	JAR			F	Alter	+ fam	YB	S
EPSTEIN	wife	JAR			M			YB	S
EPSTEIN	Alter	JAR			F	Bunem	++ 2 daug	YB	S
EPSTEIN	Arieh	JAR	Bunem	wife	M			YB	S
EPSTEIN	Ben Zion	JAR	Bunem	wife	M			YB	S
FANGER	wife	JAR			F	Genie	+ 2 child	YB	S
FANGER	Nathan	JAR			M			YB	S
FANGER	wife	JAR			F	Nathan	+ 2 child	YB	S
FEDDER	Yossef	JAR			M		+ 2 sons	YB	S
FEDER	Itzhak	JAR			M			YB	S
FEDER	Rachel	JAR			F	Itzhak	+ 3 dau	YB	S
FELZNER	Hersh	JAR			M			YB	S
FELZNER	Hannah	JAR			F	Hersh		YB	S
FELZNER	son	JAR	Hersh	Hannah	M			YB	S
FELZNER	daughter	JAR	Hersh	Hannah	F	husband	+ child	YB	S
FELZNER	husband	JAR			M			YB	S
FELZNER	Pinhas	JAR			M			YB	S
FELZNER	Feitche	JAR			F	Pinhas		YB	S
FELZNER	Golde	JAR	Pinhas	Feitche	F	husband	+ child	YB	S
FELZNER	Awraham	JAR			M			YB	S
FELZNER	Hannah	JAR			F	Awraha		YB	S
FENNIK	Itamar	JAR			M			YB	S
FENNIK	wife	JAR			F	Itamar	+ sons	YB	S
FENNIK	Eisik	JAR			M			YB	S
FENNIK	Sarah	JAR			F	Eisik	++ 5 child	YB	S
FENNIK	Yossef	JAR			M			YB	S
FENNIK	Taube	JAR			F	Yossef	+ 2 child	YB	S
FENNIK	Moshe	JAR			M			YB	S
FENNIK	Henia Sar	JAR			F	Moshe	+ 3 child	YB	S
FIGER	Dawid	JAR			M			YB	S
FIGER	wife	JAR			F	Dawid	+ 3 child	YB	S
FIGER	Yoske	JAR			M			YB	S
FIGER	son	JAR	Yoske		M			YB	S

Surname	Given name	Town		Relation	Sex	Of	Add'l	Src	
FIGER	wife	JAR			F	son	+ 3 child	YB	S
FIGER	Itzhak	JAR			M			YB	S
FINGERHOIT		JAR			M			YB	S
FINGERHOIT	Feige	JAR			F	Yossef A	+ 3 child	YB	S
FINKE	Ethel	JAR			F			YB	S
FLASHNER	Ozer	JAR			M			YB	S
FLEHR	Aaron	JAR			M			YB	S
FLEHR	Sarah	JAR			F	Aaron		YB	S
FLEHR	Hantche	JAR			F		+ 2 child	YB	S
FLEHR	Yehoshua	JAR			M			YB	S
FLEHR	Frimtche	JAR			F	Yehoshu	+ 2 child	YB	S
FLEHR	Yentche	JAR			F			YB	S
FLEHR	daughter	JAR		Yentche	F	husband	+ child	YB	S
FLEHR	husband	JAR			M			YB	S
FLEHR	Malka	JAR			F		+ 5 child	YB	S
FLEHR	Keile	JAR			F			YB	S
FLEHR	Reuven	JAR			M			YB	S
FLEISHER	Artche	JAR			M			YB	S
FLEISHER		JAR			F	Artche		YB	S
FLEISHER	Moshe	JAR			M			YB	S
FLEISHER	wife	JAR			F	Moshe	+ 2 chil	YB	S
FLEISHER	Itche	JAR			M			YB	S
FLEISHER	Sarah	JAR			F	Itche	+ 6 child	YB	S
FLEISHER	Alte	JAR			F			YB	S
FLEISHER	Moshe	JAR		Alte	M			YB	S
FLEISHER	wife	JAR			F	Moshe	+ 4 child	YB	S
FLEISHER	Berish	JAR			M			YB	S
FLEISHER	Zelde	JAR			F	Berish		YB	S
FLEISHER	Dawid	JAR			M			YB	S
FLEISHER	Frimet	JAR			F	Dawid	+ 2 child	YB	S
FLEISHER	Hershel	JAR			M			YB	S
FLEISHER	wife	JAR			F	Hershel	+ 2 child	YB	S
FLEISHER	Hanntche	JAR			F		+ fam	YB	S
FLEISHER	Yossef	JAR			M			YB	S
FLEISHER	Hinde	JAR			F	Yossef	+d 6 child	YB	S
FLEISHER	Moshe	JAR			M			YB	S
FLEISHER	Pearl	JAR			F	Moshe	+ 3 child	YB	S
FLEISHER	Meir	JAR			M			YB	S

Surname	Given name	Town	Father	Mother	Sex	Spouse	Notes	Source	
FLEISHER	Baltche	JAR			F	Meir	+ 5 child	YB	S
FLEISHER	Michael	JAR			M			YB	S
FLEISHER	Fridze	JAR			F	Michael	+ 6 child	YB	S
FLEISHER	Mendil	JAR			F		+ fam	YB	S
FLEISHER	Rechel	JAR			F	husband	+ child	YB	S
FLEISHER	husband	JAR			M			YB	S
FLEISHNER	Ozer	JAR			M			YB	S
FLIGELMAN	Wolf	JAR			M			YB	S
FOGEL	Israel Yos	JAR			M		+ 4 child	YB	S
FRENKEL	Eisik	JAR			M			YB	S
FRENKEL	wife	JAR			F	Eisik	+ child	YB	S
FRIDEL	Haim	JAR			M			YB	S
FRIDEL	Sarah	JAR			F	Haim		YB	S
FRIEDMAN	Itche	JAR			M			YB	S
FRIEDMAN	Moshe	JAR			M			YB	S
FRIEDMAN	Libe	JAR			F	Moshe	+ child	YB	S
FRIEDMANN	Eltche	JAR			M			YB	S
GASTENBAUER	husband	JAR			M			YB	S
GASTENBAUER	Libe	JAR			F	husband	+ child	YB	S
GEITESMAN	Haim	JAR			M			YB	S
GEITESMAN	wife	JAR			F	Haim	+ child	YB	S
GELBER	Israel	JAR			M			YB	S
GELBER	wife	JAR			F	Israel	+ child	YB	S
GERSTEL	Meir	JAR			M			YB	S
GERSTEL	Leah	JAR			F	Meir		YB	S
GERSTEL	Shmuel	JAR	Meir	Leah	M			YB	S
GERSTEL	Yentche	JAR			F			YB	S
GERSTEL	Nachman	JAR		Yentche	M			YB	S
GERSTEL		JAR		Yentche	M			YB	S
GERSTEL	Elimelech	JAR			M			YB	S
GERSTEL	Yehoshua	JAR	Elimelec		M			YB	S
GERSTEL	Feiwel	JAR	Elimelec		M			YB	S
GERSTEL	Gittel	JAR	Elimelec		F	husband	+ child	YB	S
GERSTEL	husband	JAR			M			YB	S
GERSTEL	Yeshua	JAR			M			YB	S
GERSTEL	wife	JAR			F	Yeshua	+ child	YB	S
GERSTEL	Shalom	JAR			M			YB	S
GERSTEL	Hudes	JAR			F	Shalom		YB	S

Surname	Given Name	Town	Rel1	Rel2	Sex	Related	Notes	Src1	Src2
GERSTEL	Tzvi Nat	JAR			M			YB	S
GERSTEL	wife	JAR			F	Tzvi Nat	and childr	YB	S
GERSTEL	Mordecha	JAR			M			YB	S
GERSTEL	Moshe	JAR			M			YB	S
GERSTEL	wife	JAR			F	Moshe	+ 2 child	YB	S
GERSTEL	Yossef	JAR			M			YB	S
GERSTEL	wife	JAR			F	wife		YB	S
GERSTEL	son	JAR	Yossef	wife	M			YB	S
GISSER	Dawid	JAR			M			YB	S
GISSER	Zelig	JAR			M			YB	S
GISSER	Sarah	JAR			F	Zelig	+ child	YB	S
GISSER	Feiwel	JAR			M			YB	S
GISSER	Yaakow	JAR			M			YB	S
GISSER	wife	JAR			F	Yaakow	+ 2 child	YB	S
GISSER	Yaakow	JAR			M		+ fam	YB	S
GISSER	Leib	JAR			M			YB	S
GISSER	Ethel	JAR			F	Leib	+ 3 child	YB	S
GISSER	Pithiya	JAR			M			YB	S
GISSER	Israel	JAR			M			YB	S
GISSER	Rishe	JAR			F	Israel	+ child	YB	S
GISSER	Sarah	JAR			F			YB	S
GISSER	Sheindele	JAR			F			YB	S
GOLD	Yossef	JAR			M			YB	S
GOLD	Miriam	JAR			F	Yossef	+ fam	YB	S
GOLDSHTECHER	Haya	JAR			F			YB	S
GOLDSTEIN	Shmuel	JAR			M			YB	S
GOLDSTEIN	Riwka	JAR			F	Shmuel	+ 2 sons	YB	S
GRINWALD	Israel Wo	JAR			M			YB	S
GRINWALD	Yossef	JAR			M			YB	S
GRINWALD	Moshe	JAR			M			YB	S
GRINWALD	wife	JAR			F	Moshe	+ child	YB	S
GRINWALD	Israel Wol	JAR			M			YB	S
GRINWALD	wife	JAR			F	Israel W	+ child	YB	S
GRINWALD	Leib	JAR			M			YB	S
GRINWALD	wife	JAR			F	Leib	+ child	YB	S
GROS	Fryda	JAR			F			YB	S
GROSS	Leib	JAR		Shifra	M			YB	S
GROSS	Meir	JAR			M			YB	S

GROSS	Yossef	JAR		M			YB S
GROSS	Dawid	JAR		M		+ fam	YB S
GROSS	Zelig	JAR		M			YB S
GROSS	Gitel	JAR		F	Zelig		YB S
GROSS	Haya She	JAR		F			YB S
GROSS	Riwkah	JAR		F			YB S
GROSS	Fristche	JAR		F			YB S
GROSS	Yehudith	JAR		F			YB S
GROSS	Yaakow	JAR		M			YB S
GROSS	wife	JAR		F	Yaakow	+childr	YB S
GROSS	Yankel	JAR		M			YB S
GROSS	Yentele	JAR		F	husband		YB S
GROSS	husband	JAR		M			YB S
GROSS	Yaakow	JAR		M			YB S
GROSS	wife	JAR		F	Yaakow	+ 3 child	YB S
GROSS	Lewy	JAR		M			YB S
GROSS	wife	JAR		F	Shimeon	+ child	YB S
GROSS	Dawid	JAR		M			YB S
GROSS	wife	JAR		F	Dawid		YB S
GROSS	Rella	JAR		F			YB S
GROSS	Arieh	JAR		M			YB S
GROSSHTERN	Itzhak	JAR		M			YB S
GUTTHERTZ	Husband	JAR		M			YB S
GUTTHERTZ	Haya Sar	JAR		F	Husband		YB S
HABERCORN		JAR		M			YB S
HABERCORN	wife	JAR		F	Shmuel Ber		YB S
HABERCORN	Moshe	JAR		M			YB S
HABERCORN	wife	JAR		F	Moshe		YB S
HAHN	Yekel	JAR		M			YB S
HAHN	wife	JAR		F	Yekel	+ fam	YB S
HAHN	Shmuel B	JAR		M			YB S
HAHN	wife	JAR		F	Shmuel	+ 4 child	YB S
HALPERN	Beile Rac	JAR		F			YB S
HALPERN	daughter	JAR	Beile Ra	F		+ 4 child	YB S
HALPERN	Henich	JAR		M			YB S
HALPERN	wife	JAR		F	Henich	+ child	YB S
HALPERN	Moshe	JAR		M		+ fam	YB S
HALPERN	Itzhak	JAR		M			YB S

Surname	Given name	Town	Father	Mother	Sex	Spouse	Other	Source	
HALPERN	Eliy wife	JAR			F	Itzhak Eli	+ child	YB	S
HANDELSMAN	Esther Tzi	JAR			F			YB	S
HANDELSMAN	Awigdor	JAR			M	Awigdor		YB	S
HANDELSMAN	Gitel	JAR	Awigdor	Esther T	F			YB	S
HANDELSMAN	Adel	JAR	Awigdor	Esther T	F	husband	+ 2 child	YB	S
HANDELSMAN	Shalom	JAR	Awigdor	Esther T	M			YB	S
HANDELSMAN		JAR			M		+ fam	YB	S
HARDES	Motie	JAR			M			YB	S
HARDES	wife	JAR			F	Motie	+ child	YB	S
HASS	Fishel	JAR			M			YB	S
HASS	Tzwete	JAR			F	Fishel		YB	S
HAWA		JAR			F		+ 8 child	YB	S
HAYA	Sheindel	JAR			F	Mordechai Ber		YB	S
HAYA		JAR			M			YB	S
HECHT	Ben Zion	JAR			M			YB	S
HECHT	wife	JAR			F	Ben Zion	+ child	YB	S
HECHT	Yossef	JAR			M			YB	S
HECHT	son	JAR	Yossef		M			YB	S
HECHT	daughter	JAR	Yossef		F			YB	S
HINDA		JAR			F			YB	S
HIRSHORN		JAR			M			YB	S
HIRSHORN	Reisel	JAR			F	Israel Moshe	+ 2 child	YB	S
HITZ	Alter	JAR			M			YB	S
HITZ	Hawa	JAR			F	Alter		YB	S
HITZ	son	JAR	Alter	Hawa	M			YB	S
HITZ	Leizer	JAR			M			YB	S
HITZ	wife	JAR			F		+ child	YB	S
HITZ	Frida	JAR			F	husband		YB	S
HITZ	husband	JAR			M			YB	S
HITZ		JAR			M			YB	S
HOCHBERG	Eliyahu Z	JAR			M			YB	S
HOCHBERG	son	JAR	Eliyahu Zal		M		+ fam	YB	S
HOCHBERG	Abale	JAR			M			YB	S
HOCHBERG	Mindel	JAR			F	Abale	+ 4 child	YB	S
HOCHBERG	Dawid	JAR			M			YB	S
HOCHBERG	Hannah	JAR			F	Dawid		YB	S
HOCHBERG	Zalman	JAR			M			YB	S

HOCHBERG	daughter	JAR	Zalman		F	Zalman	+ child	YB	S
HOCHBERG	husband	JAR			M			YB	S
HOCHBERG	Moshe	JAR	Zalman		M		+ 6 child	YB	S
HOCHBERG	Zelig	JAR			M			YB	S
HOCHBERG	Riwtche	JAR			F	Riwtche		YB	S
HOCHBERG	Awraham	JAR	Zelig	Riwtche	M			YB	S
HOCHBERG	Pearl	JAR			F	Awraha	+ child	YB	S
HOCHBERG	Itzhak	JAR			M			YB	S
HOCHBERG	Feige	JAR			F	Itzhak	+6 child	YB	S
HOCHBERG	Golda	JAR	Itzhak		F	husband		YB	S
HOCHBERG	husband	JAR			M			YB	S
HOCHBERG	Leib	JAR			M			YB	S
HOCHBERG	son	JAR	Leib		M			YB	S
HOCHBERG	Leibish	JAR			M			YB	S
HOCHBERG	Sarah	JAR	Leibish		F	husband	+ 2 child	YB	S
HOCHBERG	husband	JAR			M		+2 child	YB	S
HOCHBERG	Lawish	JAR			M			YB	S
HOCHBERG	Motel	JAR			M			YB	S
HOCHBERG	Tzipe	JAR			F	Motel		YB	S
HOCHBERG	Moshe	JAR			M			YB	S
HOCHBERG	wife	JAR			F	Moshe	+ child	YB	S
HOCHBERG	Aaron	JAR			M			YB	S
HOCHBERG	Yente	JAR			F	Aaron	+ 6 child	YB	S
HOCHBERG	Leibish	JAR			M			YB	S
HOCHBERG	Feige	JAR			F	Leibish		YB	S
HOCHBERG		JAR			M			YB	S
HOCHBERG	Mordecha	JAR			M			YB	S
HOCHBERG	Aaron	JAR	Mordech		M			YB	S
HOCHBERG	Zakman	JAR	Mordech		M			YB	S
HOCHBERG	Itche	JAR			M			YB	S
HOCHBERG	Yente	JAR			F	Itche	+3 child	YB	S
HOCHBERG	Yossef	JAR			M			YB	S
HOCHBERG	Leibish	JAR			M			YB	S
HOCHBERG		JAR	Leibish		F			YB	S
HONIK	Hannah	JAR			F			YB	S
HONIK	Yekel	JAR		Hannah	M			YB	S
HONIK	Salke	JAR			F	Yekel	+2 child	YB	S
HONIK	Mirtche	JAR		Hannah	F	Shmuel	+ 2 child	YB	S

HONIK	Shmuel	JAR			M			YB	S
HOROWITZ	Elimelech	JAR			M			YB	S
INDIK	Eliyahu	JAR			M			YB	S
INDIK	wife	JAR			F	Eliyahu	+ child	YB	S
INDIK	Awrahm	JAR			M			YB	S
INDIK	wife	JAR			F			YB	S
INDIK	Shaul	JAR	Awrahm	wife	M			YB	S
INDIK	Motie	JAR			M			YB	S
INDIK	wife	JAR			F	Motie		YB	S
INDIK	Yossef	JAR			M			YB	S
INDIK	Klara	JAR			F			YB	S
INDIK	Ida	JAR			F			YB	S
INDIK	Leon	JAR			M			YB	S
INDIK	Maria	JAR			F			YB	S
ITZHAK	Eisik	JAR			M			YB	S
ITZHAK	Henie	JAR			F	Eisik		YB	S
ITZHAK	Yokel	JAR	Eisik		M			YB	S
KAHANE	Mendil	JAR			M			YB	S
KAHANE	wife	JAR			F		+2 child	YB	S
KAHANE	son	JAR	Mendil	wife	M			YB	S
KAHANE	wife	JAR			F	son	+ fam	YB	S
KAHANE		JAR			M			YB	S
KAHANE	Yuta	JAR			F	Yeshayahu		YB	S
KAHANE	Esther	JAR	Yeshaya	Yuta	F		+ 2 child	YB	S
KANNER	Herman	JAR			M			YB	S
KASSEL	Hiel	JAR			M			YB	S
KASSEL	Jona	JAR			M			YB	S
KASSEL	Ita	JAR			F			YB	S
KASSEL	Majer	JAR			M			YB	S
KASSEL	Tzipe	JAR			F			YB	S
KASSEL	Josel	JAR			M			YB	S
KASSEL	Aron	JAR			M			YB	S
KASSEL	Adele	JAR			F			YB	S
KASSEL	Getzel	JAR			M			YB	S
KASSNER	Yoseef	JAR			M			YB	S
KASSNER	wife	JAR			F	Yoseef	+ child	YB	S
KASTNER	Leah Dr	JAR			F		+ fam	YB	S
KASTNER	Yossef	JAR			M			YB	S

Surname	Given Name	Town	Father	Mother	Sex	Spouse	Notes	Source
KASTNER	son	JAR	Yossef		M			YB S
KATZ	Bertche	JAR			M			YB S
KATZ	Tziril	JAR			F	Bertche		YB S
KATZ	Malka	JAR			F			YB S
KATZ	Malka	JAR			F		+5 child	YB S
KATZ		JAR			M			YB S
KATZ	Shmuel	JAR			M			YB S
KATZ	Shlomtzi	JAR			M			YB S
KATZ	Sarah Ri	JAR			F			YB S
KATZ	Taube	JAR		Sarah Ri	F			YB S
KATZ	brother	JAR		Sarah Ri	M			YB S
KAUFMAN	Kreintche	JAR			F			YB S
KEHR	Aaron	JAR			M			YB S
KEHR	wife	JAR			F	Aaron	+4 child	YB S
KEHR	Eliyahu	JAR			M			YB S
KEHR	wife	JAR			F	Eliyahu	+ child	YB S
KEHR	Berish	JAR			M		+ child	YB S
KEHR	wife	JAR			F	Berish		YB S
KEHR	Haim	JAR			M			YB S
KEHR	Roize	JAR			F	Haim	+ fam	YB S
KEHR	Alter Sha	JAR			M			YB S
KEHR	Wigdor	JAR			M			YB S
KEHR	Rishe	JAR			F	Wigdor	+ 3 child	YB S
KERNER		JAR			M			YB S
KERNER	Hannah	JAR			F	Moshe Y		YB S
KERNER		JAR	Moshe Y	Hannah	M			YB S
KERNER	wife	JAR			F	Awramtc	+ child	YB S
KESSEL	Chana	JAR			F			YB S
KESSEL	Mechel	JAR			M			YB S
KESSEL	Henoch	JAR			M			YB S
KESSEL	Rachel	JAR			F			YB S
KESTLER	M	JAR			M			YB S
KEZ	Yehiel	JAR			M			YB S
KEZ	Frida	JAR			F	Yehiel	+fam	YB S
KEZ	Nachman	JAR			M			YB S
KEZ	wife	JAR			F	Nachman	+ 2 child	YB S
KEZ	Noach	JAR			M			YB S
KEZ	wife	JAR			F	Noach	+ 9 child	YB S

Surname	Given name	Place	Father	Mother	Sex	Spouse	Other	Source
KEZ	Riwkah	JAR			F	Shimon		YB S
KEZ	Shimon	JAR			M			YB S
KEZ	son	JAR	Shimon	Riwkah	M			YB S
KEZ	Pessah	JAR			M			YB S
KIMMEL	Golde	JAR			F			YB S
KIMMEL	daughter	JAR		Golde	F			YB S
KIMMEL	Hersh	JAR			M			YB S
KIMMEL	wife	JAR			F	Hersh	+ 2 child	YB S
KIMMEL	Hersh	JAR			M			YB S
KIMMEL	Mintche	JAR			F	Hersh		YB S
KIMMEL	son	JAR	Hersh	Mintche	M			YB S
KIMMEL	wife	JAR			F	son		YB S
KIMMEL	Hannah	JAR			F		+ 3 child	YB S
KIMMEL	Yaakow	JAR			M			YB S
KIMMEL	daughter	JAR	Yaakow		F	husband	+ 2 child	YB S
KIMMEL	husband	JAR			M			YB S
KIMMEL	Yetchi	JAR			F		+ fam	YB S
KIMMEL	Yaakow	JAR			M			YB S
KIMMEL	Beile	JAR			F	Yaakow		YB S
KIMMEL	Frida	JAR	Yaakow	Beile	F	husband	+ 2 child	YB S
KIMMEL	husband	JAR			M			YB S
KIMMEL		JAR	Yaakow	Beile	F	Dawid		YB S
KIMMEL	Dawid	JAR			M		+ 2 child	YB S
KIMMEL	Meir	JAR			M			YB S
KIMMEL	wife	JAR			F	Meir	+ 7 child	YB S
KIMMEL	Moshe	JAR			M			YB S
KIMMEL	Neshe	JAR			F	Moshe	+ 3 child	YB S
KIMMEL	Fishel	JAR			M			YB S
KIMMEL	Golde	JAR			F	Fishel		YB S
KIMMEL	Zelig	JAR	Fishel	Golde	M		+ child	YB S
KIMMEL	Dawid	JAR			M			YB S
KIMMEL	Haim	JAR			M			YB S
KIMMEL	Yaakow	JAR			M			YB S
KIRCHNER	husband	JAR			M			YB S
KIRSCHNER	husband	JAR			M			YB S
KIRSCHNER	Adel	JAR			F	husband	+ 2 child	YB S
KLAPP	Awraham	JAR			M			YB S
KLEIN	Dawid	JAR			M			YB S

KNOCHN	Dawid	JAR			M			YB S
KONINGSBERG	Yaakow	JAR			M			YB S
KONINGSBERG	Czarne	JAR			F	Yaakow		YB S
KONINGSBERG	Lewy	JAR	Yaakow	Czarne	M			YB S
KONINGSBERG	Sheba	JAR	Yaakow	Czarne	M			YB S
KORFEL	Ethel	JAR			F			YB S
KORFEL	son	JAR		Ethel	M			YB S
KRANER	Haim	JAR			M		+ 3 sons	YB S
KRANER	Yantche	JAR			F		+ fam	YB S
KRANER	Rachele	JAR			F			YB S
KRANER	daughter	JAR		Rachele	F			YB S
KREINER	Yashe	JAR			M			YB S
KREINER	wife	JAR			F	Yashe	+ 3 child	YB S
KRIEG	Yakow	JAR			M			YB S
KRIEG	Yuta	JAR			F	Yakow	+ 4 child	YB S
KRIEG	Nathan	JAR			M			YB S
KRIEG	Leib	JAR			M			YB S
KRISTAL	Malka	JAR			F			YB S
KRISTAL	Benyamin	JAR		Malka	M			YB S
KRISTAL	Riwka	JAR		Malka	F			YB S
KRISTAL	Sarah	JAR		Malka	F			YB S
KRUMFER	Yona	JAR			M			YB S
KRUMFER	daughter	JAR	Yona		F	husband	+3 child	YB S
KRUMFER	husband	JAR			M			YB S
KRUMFER	Feige	JAR			F			YB S
KRUMFER	son	JAR		Feige	M			YB S
KUPERBERG	Haim	JAR			M			YB S
KUPERBERG	wife	JAR			F	Haim	+ 3 sons	YB S
KUPPERMAN	Moshe	JAR			M			YB S
LACHER	Leizer	JAR			M			YB S
LACHER	Haim Wo	JAR			M			YB S
LACHER	wife	JAR			F		+ 3 child	YB S
LACHER	Berish	JAR			M			YB S
LACHER	Tzipe	JAR			F		+ 4 child	YB S
LACHER	Yochewe	JAR			F			YB S
LACHER	Yossef	JAR		Yochewe	M			YB S
LACHER	Nahum	JAR			M			YB S
LACHER	wife	JAR			F	Nahum		YB S

Surname	Given		Father	Mother	Sex	Spouse	Other	Src
LACHER	daughter	JAR	Nahum	wife	F			YB S
LACHER	Shaul	JAR			M			YB S
LACHER	Hannah	JAR			F	Shaul		YB S
LACHER		JAR			F			YB S
LACHER		JAR			F			YB S
LACHER	Bernard	JAR			M			YB S
LACHER		JAR			M			YB S
LACKMAN	Rachel	JAR			F			YB S
LAKSAN	Raphael	JAR			M			YB S
LAKSAN	Peshe	JAR			F			YB S
LAKSAN	Gitel	JAR	Raphael	Peshe	F			YB S
LAKSAN	Hannah	JAR	Raphael	Peshe	F			YB S
LANDAU	Moshe	JAR			M			YB S
LANDAU	Kreintche	JAR			F	Moshe		YB S
LANDAU	daughter	JAR	Moshe	Kreintch	F			YB S
LANDAU	Ethel	JAR			F		+ 3 child	YB S
LANDAU		JAR			F	husband	+ 2 child	YB S
LANDAU	husband	JAR			M			YB S
LANDAU	Esther	JAR	husband	Haya Ra	F	husband		YB S
LANDAU	husband	JAR			M			YB S
LANDAU	Zishe	JAR			M			YB S
LATT	Dawid	JAR			M			YB S
LATT	Pearl	JAR			F			YB S
LATT	Miriam	JAR			F			YB S
LATT	Yossef	JAR			M			YB S
LATT	Wolf	JAR			M		+ fam	YB S
LATT	Haya	JAR			F		+ child	YB S
LATT	Awraham	JAR			M			YB S
LATT	Hannah	JAR			F			YB S
LATT	Aaron	JAR			M			YB S
LATT	husband	JAR			M			YB S
LATT	Malka	JAR			F			YB S
LATT		JAR			M			YB S
LATT	Sarah	JAR			F	Meir Leibi		YB S
LATT	Tzipe	JAR	Meir Leib	Sarah	F			YB S
LATT	Yossef	JAR	Meir Leib	Sarah	M			YB S
LATT	Baruch	JAR	Meir Lei	Sarah	M			YB S
LATT	Mendel	JAR	Meir Leib	Sarah	M			YB S

Surname	Given		Father	Mother	Sex	Spouse	Notes	Source
LATT	Frida	JAR	Meir Leib	Sarah	F			YB S
LATT	Sarah	JAR	Meir Leib	Sarah	F			YB S
LATT	Aaron	JAR			M			YB S
LATT	Awraham	JAR			M			YB S
LATT		JAR			F			YB S
LATT		JAR			M			YB S
LATT	Yossef	JAR			M			YB S
LATT	Tzirel	JAR			F			YB S
LATT	Moshe	JAR			M			YB S
LATT	Elle	JAR			M			YB S
LATT	Sarah	JAR			F			YB S
LATT	Meir	JAR			M			YB S
LATZ	Yaakow	JAR			M			YB S
LATZ		JAR			F	Yaakow		YB S
LATZ	daughter	JAR	Yaakow	Hannah	F			YB S
LEON	Yaakow	JAR			M			YB S
LERNER	Vhumi	JAR			F			YB S
LEWENBERG	Nachman	JAR			M			YB S
LEWENBERG	Miriam Sa	JAR			F	Nachma	+ 3 child	YB S
LEWENBERG	Sarah	JAR			F			YB S
LEWENBERG	daughter	JAR		Sarah	F	husband		YB S
LEWENBERG	husband	JAR			M			YB S
LEWENBERG	Pithiyahu	JAR			M			YB S
LEWENBERG	wife	JAR			F	Pithiyahu		YB S
LEWENKRON	Shmuel	JAR	Berl	Peshe	M			YB S
LIBES	Awraham	JAR			M		+ fam	YB S
LIBES	Feige	JAR			F	husband	+ fam	YB S
LIBES	husband	JAR			M			YB S
LIBES	Meir	JAR			M			YB S
LIBES	wife	JAR			F	Meir	+ 3 child	YB S
LIBES	Eisik	JAR			M			YB S
LIBES	wife	JAR			F	Eisik	+ 3 child	YB S
LIEBERMAN	husband	JAR			M			YB S
LIEBERMAN	Esther	JAR			F	husband		YB S
MANDEL	Yentche	JAR			F	Shmuel	+ 7 childr	YB S
MARSH	Dawid	JAR			M			YB S
MARSH	Yuta	JAR			F	Dawid		YB S
MARSH	Pupe	JAR	Dawid	Yuta	F			YB S

Galicia Yizkor Book

MARSH	husband	JAR			M			YB	S
MARSH	Rashe	JAR			F	husband	+2 child	YB	S
MEHL	Hersh	JAR			M			YB	S
MEHL	wife	JAR			F		+ child	YB	S
MEHL	Yona	JAR			M			YB	S
MEHL	wife	JAR			F		+ 5 child	YB	S
MEILECH		JAR			M			YB	S
MEILECH	Freidil	JAR	MEILEC		F		+3 child	YB	S
MEISEL	Moshe Ya	JAR			M			YB	S
MEISEL	Sheindel	JAR			F	Moshe Y	+ fam	YB	S
MESSER	Michael	JAR			M			YB	S
MESSER	wife	JAR			F	Michael	+ 2 child	YB	S
METZGER	Meir	JAR			M			YB	S
MINTZER	Yaakow	JAR			M			YB	S
MINTZER	Sheba	JAR			F		+ 3 child	YB	S
MOHRER	Moshe	JAR			M			YB	S
MOHRER	Henia	JAR			F	Moshe		YB	S
MOHRER	Dobrish	JAR	Moshe	Henia	F			YB	S
MOHRER	Sender	JAR			M			YB	S
MOHRER	Alter	JAR		mother	M			YB	S
MOHRER	mother	JAR			F			YB	S
MOHRER	Yossef	JAR			M			YB	S
MOHRER	Mintchi	JAR			F	Yossef		YB	S
MOHRER	Alter	JAR			M			YB	S
MOHRER	Aaron	JAR			M			YB	S
MOSHE		JAR			M			YB	S
MOSHE	Yossef	JAR	Moshe		M			YB	S
MOSHE	Toibe	JAR	Moshe		F			YB	S
MOSHE	Hannah	JAR	Moshe		F			YB	S
MOSHE	Uri	JAR	Moshe		M			YB	S
MOSHE	Shlomo	JAR	Moshe		M			YB	S
MOSHE	Michael	JAR	Moshe		M			YB	S
MOSHE	Deworah	JAR	Moshe		F			YB	S
MOST	Israel	JAR			M			YB	S
MOST	wife	JAR			F	Israel	+5 child	YB	S
MOST	Israel	JAR			M			YB	S
NACHT	husband	JAR			M			YB	S
NACHT	Feige	JAR			F	husband	+ child	YB	S

Surname	Given	Town	Father	Mother	Sex	Spouse	Other	Source	
NASH	Frida	JAR			F			YB	S
NEUBAUER	Hersh	JAR			M			YB	S
NEUBAUER	Hannah	JAR			F	Hersh		YB	S
PAPUY	Yosse	JAR			M		+ child	YB	S
PAPUY	Shlomo	JAR			M		+ 2 child	YB	S
PFENNIK	Sheindel	JAR			F			YB	S
PINHAS		JAR			M			YB	S
PINHAS	Yenti	JAR	Pinhas		F			YB	S
PINHAS	Liba	JAR	Pinhas		F			YB	S
PINHAS	Riwkah	JAR	Pinhas		F			YB	S
PINHAS	Risha	JAR	Pinhas		F			YB	S
PINHAS	Hannah	JAR	Pinhas		F			YB	S
PINHAS	Michael	JAR			M			YB	S
PUTCHNIK	Motie	JAR			M			YB	S
PUTCHNIK	Shifcha	JAR			F	Motie	+ 2 child	YB	S
RAPP	Dudke	JAR			M			YB	S
RAPP	daughter	JAR	Dudke		F	husband		YB	S
RAPP	husband	JAR			M			YB	S
RAPP	daughter	JAR	Dudke		F	husband	+ child	YB	S
RAPP	husband	JAR			M			YB	S
RAPPAPORT	husband	JAR			M			YB	S
RAPPAPORT	Fantche	JAR			F	husband		YB	S
RAPPAPORT	daughter	JAR	husband	Fantche	F			YB	S
RATA	Simha	JAR			M			YB	S
RATA	Moshe	JAR			M			YB	S
RATA	Shifre	JAR			F	Moshe	+ 2 child	YB	S
RATA	Meir Leib	JAR			M			YB	S
RATA	Bracha	JAR			F	Meir Leib		YB	S
RATA		JAR	Meir Leib	Bracha	M			YB	S
RATA	Betche	JAR			F	Haim S	+ child	YB	S
RATA	Haya Tzir	JAR	Meir Leib	Bracha	F	husband	+ 4 child	YB	S
RATA	husband	JAR			M			YB	S
RATA	Ezriel Bar	JAR			M			YB	S
RATA	Malka	JAR			F	Ezriel Bar		YB	S
RATA	Rachel	JAR	Ezriel Ba	Malka	F		+ 2 child	YB	S
RATZ	Artche	JAR			M			YB	S
RATZ	Rachel	JAR			F	Artche	+ 3 dau	YB	S

Surname	Given	Town		Relation	Sex	Parent/Spouse	Notes	Source	
RATZ	Rachel	JAR			F			YB	S
RATZ	son	JAR		Rachel	M			YB	S
RATZ	daughter	JAR		Rachel	F	Zelig Ber	+ child	YB	S
RATZ	Zelig Ber	JAR			M			YB	S
RATZ	Shmuel	JAR			M			YB	S
RATZ	Esther	JAR			F	Shmuel	+ 3 child	YB	S
RATZ	Dawid	JAR			M			YB	S
REINARD	Eliezer	JAR			M			YB	S
REINARD	Ratzi	JAR			F	Eliezer	+ 3 child	YB	S
REINER	Eliezer	JAR			M			YB	S
REIZER	Yossef	JAR			M			YB	S
REIZER	Riwkah	JAR			F			YB	S
REIZER	Benyamin	JAR			M			YB	S
REIZER	Itzhak	JAR			M			YB	S
REIZER	Esther	JAR			F			YB	S
REIZER	Yente	JAR			F		+ fam	YB	S
ROSENBERG	Israel	JAR			M			YB	S
ROSENBERG	Bracha	JAR			F	Israel	+ fam	YB	S
ROSENBERG	Yaakow	JAR			M			YB	S
ROSENBERG	wife	JAR			F	Yaakow	+ child	YB	S
ROSENBERG	Moshe He	JAR			M			YB	S
ROSENBERG	wife	JAR			F	Moshe He		YB	S
ROSENBERG	Wowe	JAR			M			YB	S
ROSENBERG	Riwkah	JAR			F	Wowe	+ child	YB	S
ROSENBERG	Pinhas	JAR			M			YB	S
ROSENBERG	Riwkah	JAR			F	Pinhas	+ child	YB	S
ROTH	Awrahm	JAR			M			YB	S
ROTH	Feige	JAR			F	Awrahm		YB	S
ROTH	Akiva	JAR			M			YB	S
ROTH	hannah	JAR			F	Akiva		YB	S
ROTH		JAR			M			YB	S
ROTH	wife	JAR			F	Mordechi	+ fam	YB	S
ROTH	Ezriel	JAR			M			YB	S
ROTH	wife	JAR			F	Ezriel	+ 2 child	YB	S
ROTHSTEIN	Yehuda	JAR			M			YB	S
ROTHSTEIN	Roze	JAR			F	Yehuda	+ fam	YB	S
ROTHSTEIN	Husband	JAR			M			YB	S
ROTHSTEIN	wife	JAR			F	Husband		YB	S

RUBIN	Itzhak	JAR			M			YB	S
RUBIN	Ethel	JAR			F	Itzhak	+ fam	YB	S
SAMET	Aaron	JAR			F	Awraha	+ 2 chld	YB	S
SAMET	wife	JAR			M			YB	S
SAMET	Hannahle	JAR			F	Aaron	+ child	YB	S
SAMET	Taube	JAR			F		+d 2 sons	YB	S
SAMET	Yekel	JAR			M			YB	S
SAMET	wife	JAR			F	Yekel	+ child	YB	S
SAMET	Leah	JAR			F			YB	S
SAMET	Feige	JAR			F			YB	S
SAMET		JAR			F			YB	S
SAMET	Yossef	JAR			M			YB	S
SAMET	Chaya	JAR			F			YB	S
SAMET	Rechel	JAR			F		+ 3 child	YB	S
SAMET	Rachel	JAR			F		+ fam	YB	S
SAMET	husband	JAR			M			YB	S
SAMET	Sarah	JAR			F	husband		YB	S
SAMET	Israel	JAR			M			YB	S
SAMET	wife	JAR			F	Israel		YB	S
SCHAFFER	Berish	JAR			M			YB	S
SCHAFFER	Beile	JAR			F	Berish		YB	S
SCHAFFER	son	JAR	Berish	Beile	M			YB	S
SCHAFFER	daughter	JAR	Berish	Beile	F			YB	S
SCHARER	Geshe	JAR			F			YB	S
SCHIDLOWSKI	Dawid	JAR			M			YB	S
SCHIDLOWSKI	wife	JAR			F	Dawid	+ 2 child	YB	S
SCHNAPER	Shmuel	JAR			M			YB	S
SCHNAPER	wife	JAR			F	Shmuel		YB	S
SCHNAPER	Moshe	JAR			M			YB	S
SCHNAPER	wife	JAR			F	Moshe		YB	S
SCHNAPER	Bracha	JAR			F	husband	+ child	YB	S
SCHNAPER	husband	JAR			M			YB	S
SCHNAPPER	Haim	JAR			M			YB	S
SCHNAPPER	Dina	JAR			F	Haim	+ 6 child	YB	S
SCHNAPPER	Reuven	JAR			M			YB	S
SCHNAPPER	Eidil	JAR			F	Reuven	+ 6 child	YB	S
SCHNECK	Yaakow	JAR			M		+ fam	YB	S
SCHNECK	Yudel	JAR			M		+ fam	YB	S

Surname	Given Name	Town	Father	Mother	Sex	Spouse	Other	Source1	Source2
SCHNECK	Ozer	JAR			M		+ fam	YB	S
SCHNECK	Yaakow	JAR			M			YB	S
SCHNECK	wife	JAR			F	Yaakow	+ child	YB	S
SCHUSTER	Eliezer	JAR			M			YB	S
SCHUSTER	wife	JAR			F	Eliezer	+ 5 child	YB	S
SCHUSTER	Tzwi	JAR			M		+ child	YB	S
SCHWARTZ	Yoshe Be	JAR			M			YB	S
SCHWARTZ	Malka	JAR			F	Yoshe Ber		YB	S
SCHWARTZ	daughter	JAR	Yoshe B	Malka	F	husband		YB	S
SCHWARTZ	husband	JAR			M			YB	S
SCHWARTZ	son	JAR	Yoshe B	Malka	M			YB	S
SCHWARTZ	wife	JAR			F	son	+ 5 child	YB	S
SCHWARTZ	Moshe	JAR			M			YB	S
SEGAL	Eliyahu	JAR			M			YB	S
SEGAL	Esther	JAR			F			YB	S
SEGAL	Brane	JAR			F			YB	S
SEGAL	Zigmund	JAR			F			YB	S
SEGAL	Freide	JAR			M			YB	S
SHAERER	Yente	JAR			F		+ fam	YB	S
SHAERER	Lipe	JAR			M			YB	S
SHAERER	wife	JAR			F	Lipe	+ fam	YB	S
SHAPIRO	Hersh	JAR			M			YB	S
SHEINDELE		JAR			F	husband	+ 2 child	YB	S
SHEINDELE	husband	JAR			M			YB	S
SHEPTACZ	Awraham	JAR			M		+ fam	YB	S
SHEPTACZ	Leizer	JAR			M		+ fam	YB	S
SHER	Dina	JAR			F			YB	S
SHER		JAR		Dina	F			YB	S
SHER	Leah	JAR		Dina	F			YB	S
SHER	Yashe	JAR			M			YB	S
SHER	wife	JAR			F	Yashe	+ 2 child	YB	S
SHER	Malka	JAR			F			YB	S
SHER	Witie	JAR		Malka	F	husband	+ 2 child	YB	S
SHER	husband	JAR			M			YB	S
SHER	Shalom	JAR			M			YB	S
SHER	Riwkah	JAR			F	Shalom		YB	S
SHER	Kalman	JAR			M			YB	S
SHMIRER	Hannah	JAR			F		+ 3 sons	YB	S

Surname	Given name	Town	Father	Mother	Sex	Spouse	Other	Source	
SHMIRER	Leib	JAR			M			YB	S
SHMIRER	Yehuda	JAR			M			YB	S
SHMIRER	Awraham	JAR			M			YB	S
SHMIRER	Shmuel	JAR			M			YB	S
SHMIRER	wife	JAR			F	Shmuel		YB	S
SHNECKBACH	Yaakow	JAR			M			YB	S
SHNECKBACH	Tile	JAR			F	Yaakow	+ 3 dau	YB	S
SHNECKBACH	Itzhak	JAR	Yaakow	Tile	M		+ child	YB	S
SHNEIDER	Moshe	JAR			M			YB	S
SHNEIDER	wife	JAR			F	Moshe	+ 4 child	YB	S
SHNERKEL	Moshe	JAR			M			YB	S
SHNERKEL	wife	JAR			F	Moshe		YB	S
SHNERKEL	daughter	JAR	Moshe	wife	F	husband	+ child	YB	S
SHNERKEL	husband	JAR			M			YB	S
SHNERKEL	son	JAR	Moshe	wife	M			YB	S
SHOFER	Yaakow	JAR			M			YB	S
SHOSS	Alter	JAR			M			YB	S
SHOSS	Feige	JAR			F	Alter	+3 child	YB	S
SHPATZ	Dawid	JAR			M			YB	S
SHRAGA	Buze	JAR			M			YB	S
SHRAGA	wife	JAR			F	Buze	+ child	YB	S
SHRAGA	Yossef	JAR			M			YB	S
SHRAGA	Hannah	JAR			F	Yossef		YB	S
SHRAGA	son	JAR	Yossef	Hannah	M			YB	S
SHRANK	Moshe	JAR			M			YB	S
SHTAHL	Feige	JAR			F		+ fam	YB	S
SHTEIG	Awraham	JAR			M		+ fam	YB	S
SHTEINER	Elimelech	JAR			M			YB	S
SHTEINER	Hantche	JAR			F	Elimelec	+ 3 child	YB	S
SHTEINER	Aaron	JAR			M			YB	S
SHTEINER	wife	JAR			F	Aaron	+ child	YB	S
SHTEINER	Awraham	JAR			M		+ 4 child	YB	S
SHTEINER	Elimelech	JAR			M			YB	S
SHTEINER	wife	JAR			F	Elimelec	+2 child	YB	S
SHTERNBERG	Yehoshua	JAR			M			YB	S
SHTOLTZBERG	Mendil Aa	JAR			M		+ 7 child	YB	S
SHTRANG	Wolf	JAR			M			YB	S
SHTRANG	Sarah	JAR			F	Wolf		YB	S

SHTRANG	daughter	JAR	Wolf	Sarah	F			YB S
SHTRIKER	Uri	JAR			M			YB S
SHTRIKER	wife	JAR			F	Uri	+ 3 child	YB S
SHUBS	Eliezer	JAR			M			YB S
SHUBS	Gitele	JAR	Eliezer		F	Fishel	+ 4 child	YB S
SHUBS	Fishel	JAR			M			YB S
SHUBS	Fishel	JAR			M			YB S
SHUBS	wife	JAR			F	Fishel	+ child	YB S
SIGEL	Sophia	JAR			F			YB S
SIMMELMAN	Ephraim	JAR			M			YB S
SIMMELMAN	Hannah	JAR			F		+ child	YB S
SIMMELMAN	Itche	JAR			M		+d 6 child	YB S
SIMMELMAN	Esther	JAR			F		+ 4 child	YB S
SIMMELMAN	Deworah	JAR			F		+ sons	YB S
SIMMELMAN	Yehoshua	JAR			F			YB S
SIMMELMAN	Drezel	JAR			M			YB S
SIMMELMAN	Lewy	JAR			M			YB S
SIMMELMAN		JAR			F	Lewy	+ 5 child	YB S
SIMMELMAN	Pessah	JAR			M			YB S
SIMMELMAN	Meir	JAR			M			YB S
SIMMELMAN	Yehudith	JAR			F	Meir	+ 5 child	YB S
SIROP		JAR			M			YB S
SOFFER	Awraham	JAR			F	Yehoshu	+ 2 chld	YB S
SOFFER	wife	JAR			M			YB S
SOFFER		JAR			M			YB S
SOFFER	Eti	JAR			F	Soffer		YB S
SOFFER	daughter	JAR	SOFFER	Eti	F	husband	+ child	YB S
SOFFER	husband	JAR			M			YB S
SOFFRES	Awraham	JAR			M			YB S
SOFFRES	Rachel	JAR			F	Awraha		YB S
SOFFRES	Tobi	JAR	Awraham	Rachel	F			YB S
SOFFRES	Sarah Ri	JAR	Awraham	Rachel	F			YB S
STAHL	Leib	JAR			M			YB S
STEIN		JAR			M			YB S
STEIN	Rute	JAR			F	Haim Da	+ fam	YB S
STEINER	Lipa	JAR			F	Lipa	+ child	YB S
STEINER	wife	JAR			M			YB S
STELLER	Hersh	JAR			M			YB S

STELLER	Beile	JAR		F	Hersh		YB	S
STERN	Husband	JAR		F	Husband		YB	S
STERN	Greta	JAR		F			YB	S
STOLTZBERG	Izi	JAR		M			YB	S
TALASOWSKA	Miriam	JAR		F			YB	S
TAUBE	Dawid	JAR		M			YB	S
TAUBE	wife	JAR		F	Dawid	+ child	YB	S
TAUBE	Bashe	JAR		F	husband		YB	S
TAUBE	husband	JAR		M			YB	S
TAUBE	Shkena	JAR		M			YB	S
TAUBE	wife	JAR		F	Shkena	+ 3 child	YB	S
TAUBE	William	JAR		M			YB	S
TEITELBAUM	Wolf	JAR		M			YB	S
TEITELBAUM	Bashe	JAR		F	Wolf	+ child	YB	S
TENENBAUM	Hannah	JAR		F		+ child	YB	S
TENENBAUM	Yaakow	JAR		M			YB	S
TENENBAUM	wife	JAR		F	Yaakow	+ 3 child	YB	S
TENENBAUM		JAR		M			YB	S
TENENBAUM	wife	JAR		F	Mordechai		YB	S
TENENBAUM	Yakel	JAR		M			YB	S
TENENBAUM	wife	JAR		F	Yakel	+ 3 child	YB	S
TIGER	Moshe	JAR		M			YB	S
TIGER	wife	JAR		F	Moshe	+ fam	YB	S
TIGER	Fishel	JAR		M			YB	S
TIGER	daughter	JAR	Fishel	F	Leibtche	+ child	YB	S
TIGER	Leibtche	JAR		M			YB	S
TILE	daughters	JAR		F			YB	S
TOLA	Leah	JAR		F			YB	S
TOLA	Yaakow	JAR		M			YB	S
TORN	Bela	JAR		F			YB	S
TRABER	Israel	JAR		M			YB	S
TRABER	wife	JAR		F	Israel	+ child	YB	S
TREIBER	Moshele	JAR		M			YB	S
TREIBER	wife	JAR		F	Moshele	+ 2 child	YB	S
TZEIGER	Yossef	JAR		M			YB	S
TZEIGER	Eliyahu	JAR		M			YB	S
TZIGLER	Hertz	JAR		M			YB	S
TZIGLER	Hertz	JAR		F	Hertz		YB	S

Surname	Given	Town	Father	Mother	Sex	Spouse	Other	Src1	Src2
TZIGLER	son	JAR	Hertz	Hertz	M			YB	S
TZIGLER	Israel	JAR			M			YB	S
TZIGLER	wife	JAR			F	Israel		YB	S
TZIGLER	Yaakow	JAR			M			YB	S
TZIGLER	Esther	JAR			F	Yaakow		YB	S
TZIGLER	son	JAR	Yaakow	Esther	M			YB	S
TZIGLER	son	JAR	Yaakow	Esther	M			YB	S
TZIGLER	Nathan	JAR			M			YB	S
TZIGLER	Manie	JAR			F	Nathan	+ child	YB	S
TZIGLER	Esther	JAR			F			YB	S
TZIGLER	Yaakow	JAR			M			YB	S
TZIGLER	Israel	JAR			M			YB	S
TZIGLER	Manie	JAR			F			YB	S
TZIGLER	Norbert	JAR			M			YB	S
TZUCKERBERG	Shifra	JAR			F		+ 2 child	YB	S
TZUKERBERG	Karl	JAR			M			YB	S
TZWETTER	Itzik	JAR			M			YB	S
TZWETTER	wife	JAR			F	Itzik	+ 3 child	YB	S
TZWETTI		JAR			F		+ child	YB	S
WALLA	husband	JAR			M			YB	S
WALLA	Yente	JAR			F	husband	+ 3 child	YB	S
WALLER	Awrahm	JAR			M			YB	S
WALLER	wife	JAR			F		+ 2 child	YB	S
WALLER	Yente	JAR			F			YB	S
WALLER	Meir	JAR			M			YB	S
WALLER	wife	JAR			F	Meir	and child	YB	S
WARM	Hersh	JAR			M			YB	S
WARM	Riwka	JAR			F	Hersh		YB	S
WASSER	Motie	JAR			M		+ fam	YB	S
WEINTRAUB	Hannah	JAR			F			YB	S
WEINTRAUB	niece	JAR			F			YB	S
WEINTRAUB		JAR			M			YB	S
WEINTRAUB	Yochewe	JAR	Shmuel Ber		F			YB	S
WEINTRAUB	son	JAR	Shmuel Ber		M			YB	S
WEINTRAUB	Hannah	JAR			F			YB	S
WEISSMAN	Awraham	JAR			M			YB	S
WEISSMAN	wife	JAR			F	Awrah	+ 3 child	YB	S
WEISSMAN	Peshe	JAR			F			YB	S

WEISSMAN	daughter	JAR		Peshe	F	husband	+child	YB S
WEISSMAN	husband	JAR			M			YB S
WEISSMAN	Yehuda	JAR			M			YB S
WEISSMAN	Miriam	JAR			F	Yehuda	+ 3 child	YB S
WEIZER	Ben Zion	JAR			M			YB S
WEIZER	wife	JAR			F	Ben Zion		YB S
WEIZER	Taube	JAR			F		+ 5 child	YB S
WELLNER	Raci	JAR			F	husband		YB S
WELLNER	husband	JAR			M			YB S
WELLNER	Ratzi	JAR			F	husband		YB S
WELLNER	husband	JAR			M			YB S
WELLNER	Shlomo	JAR			M			YB S
WELLNER	Ratzi Sho	JAR			F	Shlomo		YB S
WERTMAN	Moshe	JAR			M			YB S
WIENER	Haim Aw	JAR			M			YB S
WIENER	daughter	JAR	Haim Awraham		F			YB S
WINTER	Shlomo	JAR			M			YB S
WINTER	Yaakow	JAR			M			YB S
WINTER	Feige	JAR			F	Yaakow		YB S
WOLFF	Meir Shm	JAR			M			YB S
WOLFF	wife	JAR			F	Meir Sh	+ 2 child	YB S
WOLFF	Hannah	JAR		Meir Shm	F			YB S
WORTZEL	Awraham	JAR			M		+ fam	YB S
WORTZEL	Hertz	JAR			M			YB S
WORTZEL	wife	JAR			F	Hertz	+ 4 child	YB S
WORTZEL	Haim	JAR			M		+ fam	YB S
WORTZEL	Peshe	JAR			F		+ fam	YB S
YAAKOW		JAR			M			YB S
YAGGID	Uri Morde	JAR			M			YB S
YAGGID	wife	JAR			F	Uri Mor	sons	YB S
YAGGID	Aaron	JAR			M			YB S
YAGGID	wife	JAR			F	Aaron		YB S
YAGGID	Yossef	JAR			M			YB S
YAGGID		JAR	Yossef		M			YB S
YAGGID	Hannah	JAR			F	Dawid Tzwi		YB S
YAGGID	daughter	JAR	Dawid Tz	Hannah	F			YB S
YAGGID	Yehezkel	JAR	Yossef		M			YB S

Surname	Given	Place	Father/Rel	Sex	Relation	Notes	Src
YAGGID	wife	JAR		F		+ 2child	YB S
YAGGID		JAR	Yossef	M			YB S
YAGGID		JAR		F	Shragai Fei		YB S
YAGGID	Haim Mos	JAR		M			YB S
YAGGID	wife	JAR		F	Haim Moshe	+ 6 child	YB S
YAGGID	Mendel	JAR		M			YB S
YAGGID	Libe	JAR		F	Mendel	+ child	YB S
YAGGID	Dawid	JAR		M			YB S
YAGGID	Feiwish	JAR		M			YB S
YAGGID	wife	JAR		F	Feiwish	+ 7 child	YB S
YAGGID	Sarah	JAR	Zeev Wol	F			YB S
YAGGID	Ratzi	JAR		F	husband	+ 2 child	YB S
YAGGID	husband	JAR		M			YB S
YAGGID	Leib	JAR		M			YB S
YAGGID	Yochewe	JAR		F	Leib	+ 2 child	YB S
YAGGID	Ide	JAR		M			YB S
YAGGID	daughter	JAR	Ide	F			YB S
YAGGID	Iwa	JAR		F			YB S
YEKEL	Moshe	JAR		M			YB S
YEKEL	daughter	JAR	Moshe	F		+ child	YB S
YEKEL	husband	JAR		M			YB S
YOSSEL	Israel	JAR		M			YB S
YOSSEL	Leah	JAR		F	Israel	+ 4 childr	YB S
YOSSEL	Lemel Ya	JAR		M			YB S
YOSSEL	wife	JAR		F	Lemel Y	+ 4 childr	YB S
YOSSEL	Hannah	JAR	Lemel Yaakow	F		+ 2 child	YB S
YUDELE		JAR		M			YB S
YUDELE	wife	JAR		F	YUDELE		YB S
ZAMZILIG	Moshe	JAR		M			YB S
ZAMZILIG	wife	JAR		F	Moshe	+ child	YB S
ZILBERSTEIN	Leibish	JAR		M		+ 5 child	YB S
ZILBERSTEIN	Tzwi	JAR		M			YB S
ZILBERSTEIN	Arieh	JAR	Tzwi	M			YB S
ZILBERSTEIN	Sarah	JAR	Arieh	F			YB S
ZILBERSTEIN	Ratza	JAR	Arieh	F			YB S
ZILBERSTEIN	Esther	JAR	Arieh	F			YB S
ZILBERSTEIN	Hannah	JAR	Arieh	F			YB S
ZILBERSTEIN	Uri	JAR	Arieh	M			YB S

ZILBERSTEIN	Yossef Sh	JAR			M			YB S
ZILBERSTEIN	wife	JAR			F	Yossef S	+ child	YB S
ZILBERSTEIN	Uri	JAR			M			YB S
ZIMMERMAN	Harry	JAR			M			YB S
ZINGER	Itche	JAR			M		+ fam	YB S
ZINGER	Haim	JAR			M			YB S
ZINGER	wife	JAR			F	Haim	+ child	YB S
ZINGER		JAR			F			YB S
ZINGER	daughter	JAR		Gaya Ra	F	husband		YB S
ZINGER	husband	JAR			M			YB S
ZINGER	Haim	JAR			M		+ fam	YB S
ZINGER	Leizer	JAR			M			YB S
ZINGER	wife	JAR			F		+ 4 child	YB S
ZINGER	Miriam	JAR			F			YB S
ZINGER	Heneh	JAR			M			YB S
ZINGER	Riwkah	JAR	Heneh		F			YB S
ZINGER	Itche	JAR			M			YB S
ZINGER	wife her	JAR			F	Itche		YB S
ZINGER		JAR			M			YB S
ZINGER	Meir	JAR			M			YB S
ZINGER	Meilech	JAR			M			YB S
ZINGER	Leizer	JAR			M			YB S
ZITZAMER	Uri	JAR			M			YB S
ZITZAMER	wife	JAR			F		+2 child	YB S
ZITZAMER	Moshe	JAR			M			YB S
ZITZAMER	Rachel	JAR			F	Moshe		YB S
ZITZAMER	daughter	JAR	Moshe	Rachel	F			YB S
ZITZAMER	Moshe	JAR			M			YB S
ZITZAMER	Yuta Lea	JAR			F	Moshe		YB S
ZITZAMER	son	JAR	Moshe	Yuta Lea	M			YB S
ZITZAMER	Matel	JAR	Moshe	Yuta Lea	F	husband	+ child	YB S
ZITZAMER	husband	JAR			M			YB S
ZITZAMER	Tzadock	JAR			M			YB S
ZITZAMER	wife	JAR			F	Tzadock	+ 2 child	YB S
ZITZAMER	husband	JAR			M			YB S
ZITZAMER	Hannah	JAR			F	husband	+ 3 child	YB S
ZLATKES	Lewy	JAR			M			YB S
ZLATKES	Esther	JAR			F	Lewy	+3 child	YB S

Rabbi Dr. Mordechai Gerstel also listed in his memorial book Jewish victims from the nearby communities;

People from Winniki

LAST NAME	First Name	Resi	Father	Mother	G Spouse	child	YB	S
HOCHNERGER	ZELIG	Win				+3 daugh	YB	S
HOCHBERGER	Esther	Win	Zelig				YB	S
HOCHBERGER	Ethel	Win	Zelig				YB	S
HOCHBERGER	Pearl	Win	Zelig				YB	S
HOCHBERGER	Sheindel	Win					YB	S
HOCHBERGER	Pinie	Win		Sheindel		+fam	YB	S
MARSH	Wolf	Win					YB	S
MARSH	wife	Win			Wolf	+2 child	YB	S
MOHRER	Benyamin	Win					YB	S
MOHRER	Shimon	Win					YB	S
MOHRER	Shmuel	Win					YB	S
MOHRER	Rachel	Win				+2 child	YB	S
MOHRER	Reuven	Win					YB	S
MOHRER	Michal	Win					YB	S
MOHRER	Yossel	Win					YB	S
MOHRER	Henie	Win	Yossel				YB	S
MOHRER	Rasha	Win	Yossel				YB	S
MOHRER	Chaya Dobri	Win	Yossel				YB	S
MOHRER	Raisel	Win	Yossel				YB	S
MOHRER	Reuven	Win	Yossel				YB	S
MOHRER	Wolf Zeev		Yossel				YB	S
MOHRER	Zacharia	Win					YB	S
MOHRER	Rivka	Win					YB	S
MOHRER	Reuven	Win					YB	S
MOHRER	Michal	Win					YB	S
RIWKA	From Winnik	Win					YB	S

DZIEDZILOW COMMUNITY

				+3 child
ALTMAN				
ALTMAN	Tziporah			
ALTMAN	Leizer			
ALTMAN	Hudes		Leizer	+ sons
BUBER	David			
BUBER	wife		David	+3 child
BUBER	Chaya			+3 child
GELBER	Awraham			
GELBER	Miriam		Awraham	+2 child
GELBER	Israel			
GELBER	Henie			+1 child
GITTER	Yossef			
GITTER	Libe	Yosse		+3 child
GRUBBER	Riwkah			
GRUBBER	Chaya	Riwkah		
HASTEN	Gitel			+4 chil
HASTEN	Shaul	Gitel		
HASTEN	Nahum	Gitel		
HASTEN	Shmuel	Gitel		
HASTEN	Menachem	Gitel		
HASTEN	Nahum			
HASTEN	Liptche		Nahum	
KRIEG	David			
KRIEG	Riwtche			+4 child
KRIEG	Dudie from	Beninen		+ 3 child
KURTZ	Sarah			
LEITER	Yaacov			
LEITER	Rachel		Yacov	+2 child
LEWENKROWN	Wolf			+2 child
LEWENKROWN	Shlomo			
LEWENKROWN	Mindel	Shlom		
lEWENKROWN	Miriam	Shlom		
LEWENKROWN				
LEWENKROWN	Beryl			
LEWENKROWN	Pesha		Beryl	

LEWENKROWN	Itche		Beryl	Pesha	
LEWENKROWN	Frimet				
MANDEL	ShmueBhmuel			Taube	
MANDEL	Toibe Shmuel			Taube	+3 child
MENDELOWICZ	Itche				
MENDELOWICZ	Yehudit			tche	+2 child
MENDELOWICZ	tche				
MENDELOWICZ	Hawa			tche	
MENDELOWICZ	Israel Le				
MENDELOWICZ	Dwora				
NEUBAUER	Hersh				
NEUBAUER	Hannah			Hersh	+3 child
TENEBOIM	Yossef				
TENEBOIM	Hannah				+4 child
TENEBOIM	Yaacov He				
TENEBOIM	Wolf				
TENEBOIM	Yossef				
TENEBOIM	Yette				
TENEBOIM	Elikum				
TENEBOIM	Tzeitel				
TENEBOIM	Chaim				
TENEBOIM	Golde				+3 child
TENEVOIM	Nachman				
TENEVOIM	Hannah				
TZWERLING	Peretz				+4 child
WEINTRAUB	Aaron Itz				
WEINTRAUB	Rachel			Aar	

BARSZOWICE COMMUNITY

FLIGELMANN	Hersh Be				
FLIGELMANN	Wife			Hersh Be	+2 sons
KATZ	Hersh				
KATZ	Wife			Hersh	+3 child
KATZ	Leibish				
KATZ	Baruch		Leibish		

KATZ	wife		+4 child
KATZ	Menashe	Baruch	
KATZ	Wife		+2 child

Chapter IX
The Mismer family from Kulikow near Jarczow

קוּלִיקוֹב

The hamlet of Kulikow is above Nowy Jarczow

יארִיצ'וֹב נוֹבִי

New Jarczow is located above Lemberg

לבוב

Lwow-Lviv-Lemberg district. The city is marked with a large grated box.

Kulikow received the status of a city in 1431 under the name Bushats that was later changed to Kulikow. Later Kulikow was acquired by the Polish royal family of Jan Sobieski. Eventually the city was owned by the feudal Polish family of Radzwil. Kulikow was settled by Turkish and Tatar prisoners of war. They developed a fine wool carpet industry. Later, the city became famous for the special bread. The hamlet provided vegetables and eggs to Lemberg. There was no industry to speak of in the hamlet.

The Jewish population in Kulikow

Year	Jewish population	Total population
1765	300	-
1880	1124	3326
1890	1178	3400
1900	1211	3665
1910	1087	3914
1921	509	2886
1931	600	-

We notice the large Jewish growth between 1765 and 1880. The almost static Jewish population between 1890 and 1900. Following World War I, the Jewish population drops rapidly.

The Jews appear in the records of Kulikow as early as 1544. The Jewish population grows in Kulikow with the rule of the Sobieski family. By 1880, the Jewish community passes 1000 people. The growth slows down in the following years but following World War I, The Jewish population declines. The Jews basically handle the commercial interests of the city. Most of the Jews that left Kulikow during the war did not return to the city. The economic opportunities in the city were limited and the ambitious youth left the city for Lemberg, Vienna or even the United States. Kulikow had a synagogue, a cemetery and some charity organisations to help the poor. Ephraim Mismer a native of Kulikow, the son of Arieh David Mismer left Kulikow for the United States.

David Arieh Mismer was born in 1843 in Kulikow.

Anna Mismer was born in Kulikow. She married David Arieh Mismer

Ephraim Mismer was born in 1859 in Kulikow to David Arieh and AnnaMismer. Later Ephraim, was called Frank. According to a 1930 US census he came to the US around July 5, 1910.The census stated that he worked as a fruit peddler and lived at 19 Pitt Street in New York City. He died November 20, 1952 in Long Island.

Bayla or Bessie Zausmer-Mismer was born in Poland. She married Ephraim Mismer.We do not know the reason or cause but the family used the last name of Zausmer as their family name.

Ephraim and Bayla Zausmer had the following children;

Marcus Mismer, born May 30 1886 in Kulikow, Poland. He was the son of Ephraim and Bayla Mismer. He married Regina Wander in Poland.They left Kulikow and arrived in New York on January 10,1914 aboard the *President Lincoln*. He was a watchmaker. They came to the home of his father Ephraim Mismer in New Yor. Burial September 23 1973 (Queens, NY).

The gravestone of Marcus Mismer-Zausmer

Meyer Zausmer, born January 23, 1887 in Kulikow, Poland. He was the son of Ephraim and Bayla Mismer. He married Sadie (last name unknown) and had the following children; Hyman (1907-1992) Nathan (1911-1995), Sylvia (1913-2009 - In 1940 according to the census Meyer was working as a dairy producer and owned his home. He died on April 3, 1954 1954.

David Leo Zausmer, born November 24, 1890, in Kulikow, Poland. He was the son of Ephraim and Bayla Zausmer. Married Ida Greenstein (1897-1991) and had children; Myron (1918-1983), William (1921-?), Morris (1924-1940) and Janette (1927-?). In 1930 David was an owner of a hardware store. He died on July 24, 1977 (Huntington, NY).

Jennie Zausmer, born, 1894 in Kulikow, Poland. She was the daughter of Ephraim and Bayla Zaysner. She married Abraham Breindel. She died Sept. 5, 1970.

Abraham Zausmer born November 24, 1890, in Kulikow, Poland. He was the son of Ephraim and Bayla Zausmer. He married Fannie Spritzman (?-1970), had child Jean Zausmer (1919-1986).

Gussie Zausmer, born, 1894 in Kulikow, Poland. She was the daughter of Ephraim and Bayla Zaysner. She died August 23, 1969.

Morris Zausmer born, September 24 1901 in Kulikow, Poland. He was the son of Ephraim and Bayla Zausmer. He married Peril "Pauline" Sobelman (1902-1995), He had children; Harry (1924-2003), David Louis (1927-2003) and Bernard (1934-?). According to the 1930 census he was an electrician. He died June 12, 1989 (Fort Lauderdale, FL).

Rose or Rosie Zausmer, born February 17 1905 in Kulikow, Poland. She was the daughter of Ephraim and Bayla Zausmer. She died September 10, 1983.

Mismers to Osijek, Croatia

Map of Osijek, Croatia

The Town of Osijek in Croatia

The Jewish population of Osijek				
Year	Total population	Jews (families)	Jews (people)	% of the total population
1746–7		11		
1818		24		
1852		160		
1880	23,750		1,900	8
1900	23,000		2,070	8.3
1910	27,919		2,370	
1921	34,412		2,960	
1931	40,337		3,020	
1940			3,193	
1968	86,000		220	

The Jewish population reached a peak of 3,193 in 1940 just prior to the German occupation of Yugoslavia. Notice in 1968, there were about 220 Jews in Osijek.

Osijek dates back to Neolithic times, with the first known inhabitants belonging to the Illyrians and later invading Celtic tribes. The area was conquered by the Romans and the 7th legion was stationed there. With the collapse of the Roman Empire, the area underwent major upheavals, and battles, that resulted in chaotic conditions.

The earliest recorded mention of Osijek dates back to 1196. The town was a feudal property of the Kórógyi family, which retained it until 1472. The Ottoman Empire conquered the city on August 8, 1526. Following the Battle of Mohács in 1687, Osijek was liberated by the Habsburg Monarchy on September 29, 1687. Under Austrian rule the city expanded and modernized. The Austrians also encouraged German migration to the city and region. In 1809, Osijek was granted the title of a Free Royal City and during the early 19th century it was the largest city in Croatia. The city developed along the lines of other central European cities, with cultural, architectural and socio-economic influences filtering down from Vienna and Budapest.

Jews from the Austrian Empire began settling in Osijek under difficult conditions in the middle of the 18th century. They had no official right of residence until 1792. Religious services were held in the town from 1830, and the community was founded in 1845; it had 40 members in 1849. The congregation school and *ḥevra kadisha* were founded in 1857; a synagogue was built in 1867. Later the city would have two synagogues, one in the lower part of the city and one in the upper part of the city. When emancipation was granted to Jews in Croatia in 1873, the community prospered and was the largest one in Croatia until 1890.

The Jewish community was well organized and even had a variety of publications that appeared. The Zionist movement was well represented in the city, especially the youth movements such as Betar and Hashomer Hatzair. The city had a Jewish sports club called Maccabi headed by Yossef

Rosenberg and later by Andria Nag'y. The rabbis of the city were Dr. Shmuel Spitzer, Dr. Armans Kaminka; Dr. Shimon Unger perished in the Shoah as did Dr. Chaim Shtekel.

The Germans occupied most of Yugoslavia in April 1941. Parts were also occupied by Italy, Hungary and Bulgaria. Croatia became a so-called independent state under the leadership of Ante Pavelic. On April 13, 1941, the first pogrom against Jews was organized by Germans, Folksdeutsche or Croatians of German origin, and Swabians or Germans. The anti-Jewish campaign was led by the fanatic group called the Ustasha. On the day of the pogrom, they also burned the main synagogue and destroyed the Jewish cemetery in Osijek.

In June 1942 the Jewish community was ordered to build a settlement on the road to Tenje, a nearby village, where the Jews would be left unmolested. Three thousand Jews from Osijek, and later from other places in the region, were confined there; and by August 1942 they had all been sent either to the death camp of Jasenovac in Croatia or Auschwitz. Most of the survivors left for Israel. There is a small Jewish community in present day Osijek.

The Mismer Family in Osijek, Croatia

Wolf Mandel and Liba Weintraub gave birth to Rivkah Mandel. Rivka married Chaskel Figer, and they had the following children: Ephraim, Lea, Hannah, Reisel, Leib, Hersh and Rosa. Ephraim Figer and his family managed to escape the Shoah as did Leib Figer and his family. All other Figers perished in the Shoah.

Rosa Figer of Jarczow married Ephraim Mismer of Kulikow near Jarczow. Ephraim was born in 1886 in Kulikow near Jarczow to Isaac and Jente Mismer. Isaac Mismer was the son of David Arieh Mismer born in 1843 in Kulikow. Ephraim was drafted into the Austro-Hungarian army and stationed in present day Yugoslavia. He slowly managed to bring his entire family to the village of Orahovica, present day Slovenia. Several years later, the family moved to Osijek, present day Croatia. The Mismers named their first son David in honor of his grandfather David Mismer. The second son was named Arieh also named for his grandfather.

Efraim Mismer and Reisel Mismer née Figer and their family

David Arieh Mismer born in Kulikow near Jarczow, Poland

Itzhak Mismer born in Kulikow, Poland. He was the son of David Kulikow

Yente Mismer born in Kulikow, Poland. Se was the was married to Itzhak

Ephraim Mismer born in Kulikow near Jarczow on April 3, 1886. His parents were Itzhak and Yente Mismer born in Kulikow, Poland

Rosa Figer-Mismer born in Jarczow, Poland in 1885. She was married to Ephraim Mismer.

Ephraim and Roza Mizmer had the following children;

David Mismer born in Kulikow near Jarczow in 1905. He was the son Ephraim and Rosa Figer-Mismer

Leo Mismer born in Kulikow near Jarczow on April 3, 1908. He was the son Ephraim and Rosa Figer-Mismer.

Klara Mismer born in Kulikow near Jarczow iFebruary 2, 1910. She was the daughter of Ephraim and Rosa Figer-Mismer.

Berta Mismer born in Kulikow near Jarczow March 30, 1912. She was the daughter of Ephraim and Rosa Figer-Mismer.

Maja Mismer born in Kulikow near Jarczow. She was the daughter of Ephraim and Rosa Figer-Mismer. She died in her youth.

Hela Mismer Mismer born in Osijek, Croatia on 1919. She was the daughter of Ephraim and Rosa Figer-Mismer.

We already mentioned that Ephraim was drafted into the Austro-Hungarian army and stationed in present day Yugoslavia. Ephraim Mismer was born in 1886 in Kulikow near Jarczow. His wife Reisel Figer was born in Jarczow in 1885. Their oldest son, David Mismer was born in Kulikow in 1906, Leo Mismer was born April 3, 1908 in Kulikow. Klara Berta and Maja were born in Kulikow, near Jarczow. Hela Mismer was born in Orahovica, present day Slovenia. Later the family moved to Osijek, Yugoslavia, present day Croatia.

Roza Figer–Mismer

Above birth certificate of Reisel Figer born in Jarczow, Poland May 29, 1885 to Rivkah and Chaskel Figer

She was also a granddaughter of Wolf Mandel and Liba Weintraub. This document is dated 1926 in Lemberg. It was issued years after the actual birth day. This was a copy issued by the Jewish community office. Notice the date of the document issued, 1926 Lwow or Lemberg. Many Jewish marriages in Eastern Europe were performed by local rabbis who were not recognized by the civil authorities. As a result, the births of children were also not recorded. Birth certificates were needed for passports or draft boards. Then the community would issue a certificate of birth with the actual date when the copy was written.

Above marriage certicate between Roza Figer and Efraim Mismer in Jarczow

Passport issued to Ruza or Rosa Mismer to visit her parents in Poland

The information page of the passport dealing with Rosa Mismer

Roza Mismer born in 1885 in Jarczow, Poland, deported to Auschwitz Birkenau in 1942 where she was murdered. Testimony page by her son Leo Mismer

Brother of Rosa Figer born in Jarczow. Efraim Figer

Sister of Rosa Figer born in Jarczow

Efraim Mismer

Ephraim Mismer

He was born April 3,1886, in Kulikow, near Jarczow. He was the son of Itzhac and Jente Mismer. He married Roza Figer, daughter of Chaskel Figer and Rivkah Mandel. The marriage was performed by Rabbi Wolf Gerstel, Rabbi of Jarczow. The Austrian authorities did not recognize Jewish religious marriage ceremonies and therefore did not record the event. The Mismers were not considered married by the Austrian authorities. This practice was common among Jews in Eastern Europe. A birth and marriage certificate was needed for the draft board. Efraim Mismer obtained a marriage certificate dated September 16, 1915. The document was issued in Lwow or Lemberg. phhraim and Roza gave birth to the following children: David, Leo, Klara, Berta, Maja and Hela.

We already mentioned that the family settled in Orahovica, present day Slovenia. The village of Orahovica was small and consisted of farms and fruit orchards. There were four Jewish families in the village. Following the World War I, Efraim obtained a job as a farm supervisor. In about 1924, the family moved to Osijek, present-day Croatia, but to Osijek. The Mismer family lived modestly. With the entry of the Germans to Yugoslavia, persecution of Jews began. Germans and Croatians began to arrest Jews and sent them to detention camps and then to the death camp of Auschwitz–Birkenau.

Passport issued to Efraim Mismer when he visited his parents in Jarczow Poland.
Notice the personal information in the document.

Testimony page submitted by Leo Mismer for his father Efraim Mismer

Efraim and Roza's children

David Mismer

David Mismer

David Mismer was born in 1905 in Kulikow, near Jarczow, Poland. He grew up in Orahovica, present day Slovenia. Later the family moved to Osijek, Yugoslavia, present day Croatia. He was arrested in Osijek and sent to the Jasenovac death camp in Croatia where he was killed during the Shoah. He was married to a non-Jewish woman and had a son. They survived the war.

Testimony page for David Mismer killed in Jasenovac death camp in Croatia

Leo Mismer

Leo Arieh Mismer

Leo Mismer was born in Kulikow near Jarczow, Poland on April 3, 1908. He grew up in Orahovica, present–day Slovenia. He attended the local primary school for four years, followed by another four years of schooling, then entered the gymnasia where he studied a further four years. He graduated in 1928 and started to work in the wood industry. In 1931 he changed his job and joined the Bernard Gutman company where he worked in the office. He was exempt from military duty due to a heart condition. He met and married Mira Schwartz. They were married on March 5, 1939 in Osijek.

Leo worked until April 11, 1941 when the Germans, Italians and Bulgarians attacked Yugoslavia. Leo was immediately fired from his job. The Germans created a Croatian puppet state headed by Ante Pavelic and his paramilitary force called the Ustasha. During the summer of 1941 the Ustasha ran wild in Croatia.[1] They destroyed entire villages and killed thousands of Jews and Serbs. Jewish life became meaningless. There were constant arrests, detentions and killing of Jews. The Jewish population of about 30,000 was reduced to several thousand by 1942.[2] Leo and his wife Mira began to plan their future moves when Hela Mismer, a sister of Leo, arrived at their house and told them that the Germans were looking for her. She had decided not to report and packed a bag, heading to her brother's home. There they decided on a plan of action, to head in the direction of Italy.

Birth certificate of Leo Mismer in Polish. Certificate was issued in Jarczow

Italy was no heaven for Jews but the situation was much better there than in most occupied areas under German control. Italy had a small Jewish population of about 47,000 Italian Jews and an estimated 10,000 foreign Jews.[3] Italian Jewry was well integrated into the general Italian society: Jews served in the army and there were about 15 Jewish Italian generals in the Italian army in 1938. Jews held prominent positions including professorships at the universities and judges. The status of Jews was not affected by the seizure of power by Benito Mussolini in 1922. As a matter of fact, some Jews were members of his party. Il Duce, as Mussolini called himself, even had a Jewish mistress, Margherita Sarfatti.

As fascist Italy moved closer to Nazi Germany, things began to change in the country, especially in the press that was government controlled. An anti-Jewish campaign was launched followed by the introduction of racial laws in 1938. The first act of the new policy was the closing of the Italian schools to Jewish children. The Jewish communities had to establish their own schools. Then all Jewish civil servants were dismissed from their posts, and Jewish professionals were forbidden to practice their professions. Foreign Jews were forbidden to enter Italy. Foreign Jewish residents in Italy were urged to leave the country and a number left. Their place was soon taken by Jews who entered Italy illegally or entered areas controlled by the Italian army in Yugoslavia. Italy seized these areas in April 1941. Italian border guards and soldiers did not blindly obey the anti-Jewish orders and looked the other way, enabling Jews to smuggle themselves into the desired areas.

The Mismers decided to head to the Italian-controlled areas in Yugoslavia with the hope of entering Italy. They left Osijek by train and headed to Zagreb, capital of Croatia. There they found some assistance that enabled them to travel to Susak, Croatia. The entire trip was fraught with danger because Jews were not permitted to travel on trains. Susak was already under Italian army control but the Croatian Ustasha ruled the city. The Mismers established contact with some local people who helped them on their way to Trieste, Italy.

The stay in Italy was very difficult and many a day the Mismers had no food. The Italian police arrested them and they were sent to a camp named Aprica northern Italy. Leonardo Marinelli, a commander in the Guardia di Finanza in 1943, was stationed in Tirano and was in charge of the internment camp in Aprica.[4] Life at the camp was relaxed without harassment. While the internees were not permitted to leave the camp, they received food and some were even permitted to work, including Leo Mismer who worked in the administration of the camp. The situation changed radically when Italy capitulated to the Allies on September 12, 1943. The German military reaction was swift, as large German forces moved into Italy, among them S.S. units. The internees of the camp, especially the Jews, were mortified by the news. Most of them had no money, legal papers, nor fluency in the Italian language to escape the camp. Some did manage to leave and head to the Swiss border that was closed to illegal refugees. Guides and smugglers were hired to cross the Italian–Swiss border. Once in Switzerland many refugees were returned to Italy. Some terrible scenes took place at the borders when refugees were forced to retrace their paths where the Germans were waiting for them.

The situation of Jewish refugees in Aprica was hopeless when a papal messenger, a young Italian priest named Giuseppe Carozzi, arrived at the camp and presented the commander, Leonardo Marinelli, with a letter from the Pope asking him to liberate 300 Yugoslav Jews from the internment camp and give them safe passage into Switzerland.[5] Marinelli went against strict Nazi orders forbidding Jews, prisoners of war or anyone who had not joined Benito Mussolini's northern Italian Republic of Salo from crossing the border, and that same night let them escape from the camp. Marinelli's diary states that he even ordered guards to help carry the belongings of the Jews. After four days of traveling through unbeaten paths, the prisoners, primarily led by Carozzi and another priest, Cirillo Vitalini, along with the help of Marinelli, safely managed to cross into Switzerland.

Following the escape of the Jewish prisoners, the Nazis, who had not yet mobilized in that region, began sending more and more troops there in an effort to stop illegal border crossings. They also put into effect a decree proclaiming that anyone helping the Jews would be put to death. Marinelli, seeing the approaching danger, decided it was best to leave. On September 22, 1944, Marinelli along with his family fled to Switzerland. He remained in a refugee camp until July 4, 1945.

The Mismers were apparently among the Yugoslav Jewish refugees that crossed the border relatively easily. Their testimonies indicate that they crossed the border and were received by the Swiss authorities and assigned to a labor camp. From 1943 to 1945, Switzerland admitted 38,000 Italian refugees and about 6,000 refugees of various other nationalities.[6] It is estimated that among the 44,000 refugees there were about 5,000 to 6,000 Jews. Most of the refugees came from the area of Milan and entered Switzerland via the Swiss canton of Ticino. Most of them had some sort of help as well as assistance from local guides who knew the area.

Leo Mismer found administrative work in the Swiss camp. Later he worked at a hotel as an accountant. On August 23, 1945, the Mismers boarded a special train to Yugoslavia, and arrived on August 29, 1945. The Mismers returned to Osijek, hoping to find some members of the family, but there were no survivors. Leo started to work as an accountant for the firm Pharmacia in Osijek. In 1946 Mira Mismer gave birth to a daughter named Tanja, later Tziporah. Leo and his family left Yugoslavia for Israel on December 20, 1948 aboard the ship "Radnik".

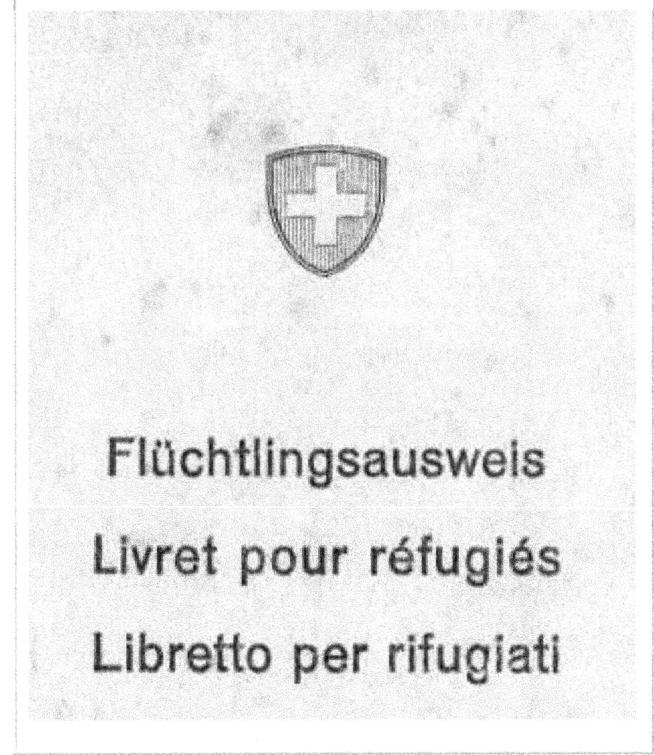

Cover page of Swiss document permitting Leo Mismer to stay in the country

Vorname / Prénom / Nome	Leo
geboren den / né le / nato il	3. April 1908
in / à / in	Zaryczow (Polen)
Staatsangehörigkeit / Nationalité / Nazionalità	Yugoslavien
Bei Staatenlosigkeit: frühere Staatszugehörigkeit / Dans les cas d'apatrides, ancienne nationalité / Per gli apolidi, nazionalità precedente	/
Beruf / Profession / Professione	Beamter
Zivilstand / Etat civil / Stato civile	verheiratet

Signalement / Connotati:

Größe / Grandeur / Statura	171 cm
Statur / Corpulence / Corporatura	mittel
Haare / Cheveux / Capelli	mittelblond
Augen / Yeux / Occhi	hellblau

Besondere Merkmale — Signes particuliers — Segni particolari

Unterschrift des Inhabers / Signature du titulaire / Firma del titolare: Leo Mismer

Swiss permit for Leo Mismer to stay in the country

Dieser Ausweis ist gültig bis
Ce livret est valable jusqu'au
Questo libretto è valido fino al

31. Dezember 1944

Bern, den
Berne, le _30. Dezember 1943_
Berna, il

Der Chef der Polizeiabteilung:
Le chef de la Division de police:
Il capo della Divisione della polizia:

i.A. Meyer

Die Gültigkeitsdauer des Ausweises wird verlängert bis
La durée de validité de ce livret est prolongée jusqu'au
La durata della validità di questo libretto viene prorogata fino al

30. Dezember 1945

Bern, den
Berne, le _30. Dezember 1944_
Berna, il

Permission to stay in Switzerland extended from 1944 to 1945

Mira Schvarz–Mismer

Mira Schvarz–Mismer

Mira Schvarz was born December 20, 1918, to Herman and Melvina Schvarz in Volpeck, Yugoslavia, a small village, where they were the only Jewish family.[7] The father had a store. Mira was an only child and the only Jewish student in her class. Several years later she moved to Osijek where her aunt lived. She finished the gymnasia in Osijek, where she met Leo Mismer and they were married on March 5, 1939. The Germans invaded Yugoslavia April 11, 1941, and set up a puppet state in Croatia that immediately began a vicious campaign aimed at the Jews. Jews were arrested, detained, sent to detention places and finally to the death camp of Jasenovac in Croatia or to Auschwitz–Birkenau. Osijek was no exception. Each day brought more arrests. Hela Mismer left her home and and joined her brother Leo Mismer and his wife in Osijek. The three Mismers decided to leave Osijek and head to Zagreb, capital of Croatia.

Here they found some help and a place to stay. They then continued their trip to Susak, Croatia. Here the atmosphere was freer because the city was occupied by the Italian Army and administered by the Ustasha administration. The Italian army did not permit ruthless brutality but still Jews were caught by the Croatians and deported to their native cities.

Mira later recalled, "We managed to contact some people and were helped to reach Trieste, Italy. We began to look for help and the Italian police arrested us but we managed to bribe our way out of jail. The second time we were arrested and sent to a special camp named Aprica.

The community of Aprica in Italy during the winter

Aprica is a town and *comune* in the province of Sondrio, Lombardy, northern Italy. It is located on the eponymous pass, the most favorable one connecting Valtellina to Val Camonica. Its main source of income is tourism, utilizing the areas geography to offer skiing in the winter and mountain biking in the summer. The area has many resort facilities that were not used during the war. The Ministry of Defense rented a facility and converted it to an illegal refugees camp for people that crossed illegally to Italy. The camp contained a large Yugoslav Jewish population. The camp was under military control but a relaxed atmosphere prevailed. The inmates were not harassed. May of them worked in the camp while others played cards or read. There was little contact between the inmates and the Italian army since most inmates did not speak Italian. This is what Mira Mismer has to say about the camp: "her sister-in-law Hela Mismer Mira and I ran a laundry operation for the wealthier residents of the camp in order to earn a few lira to be able to buy extra necessities of life. There were also social evenings in the camp."

This situation came to an abrupt end on July 25, 1943 when Benito Mussolini was dismissed from office. The Grand Council voted him out of office. He tried to enlist the help of the King of Italy but the later refused to intervene. On leaving the office he was arrested by the Italian police and placed in detention. Marshal Pietro Bagdalio was appointed Premier. September 8, 1943, Italy surreneded to the Allies and on October 13, 1943 declared war on Germany. Germany had many troops in Italy and ordered the forces to seize power. The German army took control of the country and the S.S. were out to get every Jew, Italian or forein. The Mismers saw the writing on the wall and headed on foot to Switzerland. They managed to enter the country and began to work in Switzerland and also received some food packages from the American Mismers. The latter wanted to take them to the United States following the war. The Mismers thanked the United States family but preferred to return to Osijek and look for family survivors.

```
Name:   M I Š M E R   Mira                    T/D    679 706
        geb. SCHWARZ
        Herman u. Malvine Kohn                Rel.   jüd.
Geb.:   25.3.18    Osijek                     Nat.   isr.
        4.41       verhaftet i. Osijek
        8.41       Flucht n. Susak
        2.42       Flucht n. Triest
        3.42       Zwangsaufenth. i. Aprica/Ital.
        9.43       i.d.Schweiz gefl.
        5.45       befr.?
                   Flüchtl.Lg. Engelberg/Schweiz
       20.12.48    v. Jug. n. Isr. m. "Radnik"
        BA.f.Wg.Kobl.
        f.RA. Greve, Hann.
                                                      Sch
```

Mira Schvarz–Mismer document describing in German her wanderings with her husband Leo Mismer and sister–in–law Hela Mismer during the war

According to the document, she was born March 25, 1918 to Herman and Malvina Schvarz in Osijek. In August 1941 they managed to escape and fled by train to the city of Susak, Croatia. In February 1942 they reach the city of Trieste in Italy. In March 1942, they were placed in forced detention in Aprica, Italy. In September 1943, they entered Switzerland as refugees. In May 1945, they were liberated in the refugee camp in Engelberg, Switzerland. December 12, 1948, Leo, Mira and Tanja Mismer left Yugoslavia for Israel. The family changed the name Mismer in Israel to Mizmor.

Mira's personal information

Mira Mismer's refugee status was extended from December 30, 1944, to December 30, 1945

Page of Testimony for Melvina Schwartz, mother of Mira Schwartz–Mismer killed in Auschwitz–Birkenau

Klara Mismer with her husband Imre Schlezinger

Klara Mismer

Klara Mismer was born in Kulikow near Jarczow, Poland, on February 2, 1910 and moved with her family to Orahovica, present day Slovenia. Later the family moved to Osijek where she grew up. She married Imre Schlezinger. Both were detained in Osijek and sent to Auschwitz–Birkenau where they were murdered.

Page of Testimony for Klara Mismer–Schlesinger, sister of Leo Mismer

Berta Mismer

Berta Mismer was born in Kulikow near Jarczow, Poland, on March 30, 1912 and moved with her family to Orahovica, present day Slovenia. Later the family moved to Osijek where she grew up. She married Ernest Messinger. Both were detained in Osijek and sent to Auschwitz–Birkenau where they were murdered.

Page of Testimony for Berta Mismer–Messinger, sister of Leo Mismer

Maja Mismer

Maja Mismer was born in Kulikow near Jarczow, Poland, and moved with her family to Orahovica, present day Slovenia. Later the family moved to Osijek where she grew up.

She was about 20 years old when she developed a serious ear infection, was taken to a hospital where she had surgery, and died some time later.

Hela Mismer

Hela Mismer was born Jauary 10, 1919, in Orahovica, present day Slovenia to Efraim and Roza Mismer. In 1924, the family moved to Osijek, Croatia, where she grew up. She started her education in the Jewish school and continued with the public school. She finished the gymnasia. Hela belonged to Zionist groups in Osijek including Betar, a right-wing Zionist youth movement that she did not particularly care for, and so she switched to Hashomer Hatzair, a Marxist Zionist youth movement. She attended Zagreb University and majored in Slavonic studies. She had to stop her studies due to a lack of funds. She started to work and lived in Zagreb. Shortly after the Germans occupied Osijek they searched for her but she was not home. When she reached home, her mother gave her the note that the Germans left to the effect that she had to report to the German office to begin to clean the living quarters of German officers in Osijek.

She never reported but instead packed her bag and headed to the flat of her older brother Leo and his wife Mira Mismer in Osijek. They were together until they reached Switzerland. Hela was sent to a labor camp near Zurich. Following the war the Mismers returned to Osijek, only to discover that the entire family had perished in the Shoah.

There is some repetition in the testimonies of the Mismers but we felt that the testimonies strengthen the main theme of authenticity.

Branko Kraus

Branko Kraus was born October 30, 1909, to Julius and Therese Kraus in Koprivnica, Yugoslavia. The family moved to Zagreb where he attended school, and later worked as a bookeeper. He married a non-Jewish woman, and following the German occupation of Zagreb he went into hiding until 1942. Then he decided to leave Zagreb and his wife. He headed for Italy, where he was arrested and sent to the Aprica interment camp.

```
Name:     K R A U S, Branko              T/D 972793
Eltern:   Julius u. Therese geb. HIRSCHL
Ehem.:                                        mos.
Ehefr.:   Hela geb. MISMER        Rel.:
Geb.:     30.10.1909 Koprivnica/Jug.      isr./ jugosl.
─────────────────────────────────────────────────────
Apr. 41 - Jan. 1942  Sterntr. in Zagreb, dann
                     Flucht üb. Laibach nach Aprica Prov.
                     Sondrio
bis Sept.43 Beschränkungen, dann Flucht nach der
Schweiz.Lg. in Gierenbad u. Lauffen b. Basel u.
Zweidlen/ Aug. 45 nach Zagreb/ 16.12.48 von Zagreb
üb. Fiume nach Israel mit e/s "RADNIK"
Amt f. Wg.d.L.Rhl./Pf. Berlin    Brief-Nr.:
URO Berlin/EING/ 30.6.69                 15.7.69 wa
```

The form states that his parents were Julius and Therese née Hirschl. He was married to Hela Mismer. He was born October 30, 1909 in Koprivnica, Yugoslavia. From April 1941 to January 1942 he was hidden in Zagreb. From January 1942 to September 1943 he was in the Aprica internment camp in Italy. From September 1943 to August 1945 he was in Switzerland at the following labor camps: Gierenbad, Laufen near Basle and Zweidlin.

In August 1945, he returned to Zagreb, Yugoslavia. He left Zagreb on December 16, 1948 for Israel aboard the ship *Radnik* from the port of Fiume.

Following the war, Branko returned home to find that his wife had divorced him during his absence. He met Hela Mismer and they married on September 17, 1945 in Osijek.

They emigrated to Israel, where they had two children: Dani and Irit.

Hela Mismer and Branko Kraus in Israel

Testimony page for Therese Kraus murdered in Auschwitz–Birkenau in 1942

All the Mismers lived in the village of Kulikow near Jarczow.

David Arieh Mismer had two sons: Ephraim Mismer and Itzhac Mismer.

Translator's Footnotes

1. Susan Zuccotti, The Italians and the Holocaust, Basic Publishers Inc. New York. 1987. p.77

2. Ibid., p.77

3. Zuccotti p.5

4. Marchione, Margherita, *Did Pope Pius XII Help the Jews*, Paulist Press, USA, p. 77

5. Ibid., p.77

6. Zuccotti, p. 230.

7. Mira's testimony states clearly that she was born December 20, 1918 in Volpeck, Yugoslavia. Yet her Swiss labor permit states that she was born March 25, 1918 in Osijek. We have to accept Mira's testimony as opposed to the Swiss document since we do not know what documents she showed the Swiss.

CHAPTER X
Kamionka–Strumilowa
(Kamyanka Buzka, Ukraine)
50°06' / 24°21

Kamionka–Strumilowa rynek or marketplace

The city was previously known as Kamionka– Strumilowa and was a district city in Galicia. From 1918 to 1939 it was part of Poland, and called Kamionka–Strumilowa. It is 40 km (25 miles) to the northeast of Lemberg-Lwow–Lviv. The whole area is situated in the Vistula River basin, on the Bug River.

Kamionka population

Year	Whole population	Jews
1765	(?)	522
1880	6,107	2,922
1890	6,483	3,142
1900	7,310	3,164
1910	8,106	3,549
1921	6,518	2,685
1931	(?)	3,283

The Jewish population kept growing until World War One when there was a drop in population. Following the war period, the Jewish population resumed its growth.

Kamionka is first mentioned as a village in 1448. Then its status changed to that of a city. In 1509, taxes were imposed on the trade of wine, and the money was used to build fortifications in the city. Later on, taxes were imposed on the salt merchants salt who had to remain in the hamlet for three days. In the 16th century, the city saw the formation of "guilds" or artisan associations. Fishing was an important source of income as the hamlet was situated on the River Bug that provided a means of transportation all the way to the port of Danzig. In the 19th century there were flourmills, carpentries using steam engines, a brewery, a textile plant and a brick factory in Kamionka-Strumilowa.

The first Jews appeared in Kamionka in about 1456, when two houses were owned by Jews. In 1564, a head tax was imposed on 10 Jewish home owners. In 1589, an understanding was reached between local Jews and the city leaders that Jews could build homes and conduct business without interference. The Archbishop of Lemberg, Jan Pruchnik, gave the local Jews permission to build a synagogue in 1627. The Jewish population grew during the 16th –18th centuries. They dealt in salt, trees, fish, wheat and cattle. In 1913, a big fire swept the Jewish quarter in Kamionka and most of the Jewish homes were destroyed. Soon World War One started and most Jews left the city for fear of the advancing Russian forces known for their anti-Jewish behavior. Following the war, many Kamionka Jews did not return to the city. Slowly, the Jewish community began to rebuild itself and reestablish its institutions. Religious life continued around the synagogues and the rabbis of the town. The Kamionka-Strumilowa community was very religious.

Following World War I, the Jewish workers were slowly forced out of the local work force and had no choice but to turn to small commerce: peddling, trade or artisanship. The Jewish economic situation declined rapidly. Poverty forced more and more Jews to seek social help from the Jewish population in

Kamionka. Several small banks were opened to help the Jewish economic sector. The high rate of unemployment also brought social changes among the Jewish population. Zionism appeared, especially among the Jewish youth. The Hashomer Ha-Tzair or Zionist Marxist youth movement opened a branch in the city in 1920, followed by the Poalei Tzion youth movement and the Ezra orthodox movement. The Zionist adults challenged the local religious leaders for leadership of the community. In 1927, there were four Jewish municipal counselors out of 16 members. One of the Jewish members was a Zionist. In 1931, five Jews were elected to the municipal council, two Zionists, two religious Jews and one independent. The Zionist supporters in Kamionka belonged to the General Zionists, Mizrahi and Labor. There were also Jewish communists but little is known about them since the Communist Party was banned in Poland.

Following the German attack on Poland on September 1, 1939, hundreds of Jews fled to the eastern part of Poland. Kamionka received many Jews from Western Poland. The Jewish population now grew to about 4,000 residents. The local Jewish population organized itself to help absorb the Polish Jewish refugees. On September 17, 1939, the Soviet Union attacked Poland, which was fighting the Germans. Poland collapsed and the Soviet army soon entered Kamionka-Strumilowa.

According to Israel Pasternak, a native of Kamionka, "the Soviet army entered the city followed by the Soviet secret police and the Communist Party. A local branch of the party was immediately opened in Kamionka and people were urged to join. The leadership of the city was being replaced by party members. Some of the dismissed people were arrested by the local secret police known as the N.K.V.D. All local residents were immediately converted to Soviet citizens. The Polish refugees were also urged to become Soviet citizens. All Zionist and Jewish national organizations were closed. Only the party newspaper appeared. Large places of employment were nationalized as were the banks. People began to watch themselves, as individuals were taken away at night and disappeared. Everybody was urged to get a job. Shortages of necessities became a daily occurrence. Artisans organized cooperatives. Slowly private stores went out of business because they could not replace their merchandise. Coupons were introduced for everything from bread to shoes. Pasternak started to work for the government but the pay was small and barely covered his expenses. Then one day, all refugees who refused to become Soviet citizens were rounded up and deported to the interior of the Soviet Union, mainly to Siberia. Within a short period of time, the Jewish population was economically pauperized".

Germany then attacked the Soviet Union and made great military strides. The Soviet army began to retreat and a few young Jews from Kamionka-Strumilowa joined the retreating forces, among them Israel Pasternak. He left his family and began to retreat to the depths of the Soviet Union.

The Germans occupied the city on June 28, 1941, and the next day they detained and murdered 200 Jews. July 2,1941, the local population staged an anti-Jewish pogrom with the encouragement of the Germans. The same month the Germans established the Judenrat, a Jewish council that would comply with all Gestapo requests, including cheap labor. German actions continued and a labor camp was established in the city. Jews from the nearby small villages were driven to the Kamionka-Strumilowa camp. On September 15, 1942, the big selection took place and 1,500 Jews were sent to the Belzec death camp. A few days later, 600 Jews were murdered in the vicinity of the city during another German action. Peshe Rozen, a resident of Kamionka-Strumilowa, described what happened: "The Germans went from house to house, farm to farm looking for Jews. I was hidden in a tool shed and survived the mass hunt. Within a day, I left Kamionka-Strumilowa and headed to the ghetto of Jarczow where my family was living. My husband and daughter were grabbed by the Germans and sent to Belzec".

Following these German actions, the surviving Jews began to look for hiding places and built shelters to hide in. The Germans continued to hunt for Jews and managed to round up another few hundred that were sent to Belzec. A few Jews remained in the city that worked for the German army and some cleaning details. They too were gradually murdered. Some Jews managed to escape and join the partisans. The city was liberated by the Soviet army on July 27, 1944. The city had a few Jewish survivors. Some like Peshe returned from a German labor camp in the hope of finding relatives. Then Jews began to return from the depths of the Soviet Union, among them Israel Pasternak who was very ill. She tended to him, they married and remained in Kamionka-Strumilowa. There were a few other elderly Jews in the city but most Jewish survivors left the city. Israel Pasternak and his wife Peshe Rozen-Pasternak left Kamionka-Strumilowa in 1957 for Israel.

Among the stories Israel Pasternak told of the Jewish survivors of Kamionka-Strumilowa is the story of Frank Blachman. " He was born December 11, 1922, and was 18 years old when the Germans invaded the area in 1941. Following the invasion, German officials issued regulations intended to isolate the Jews and deprive them of their livelihood.

Frank Blachman as a soldier in the Polish army

Frank Blaichman/Blachman took great risks to help his parents and family survive these hardships. With a bicycle, he rode from the neighboring farms to nearby cities, buying and selling goods at each destination. He refused to wear the Star of David armband. When word spread that the Jews of Kamionka were to be resettled in a ghetto, he hid in a bushy area outside of town. He stayed with a friendly Polish farmer and then joined other Jews hiding in a nearby forest. In the forest, the threat of being discovered was constant. Frank, recalled Israel Pasternak, encouraged the men to organize a defense unit. He obtained firearms by posing as a Polish policeman, using an overcoat he had found.

After a German attack on the partisans' encampment killed 80 Jews, the survivors left the forest to hide with sympathetic farmers. Always on the move, they killed German collaborators, destroyed telephone lines, damaged dairy factories and ambushed German patrols.

Frank's squad joined a larger all-Jewish unit, with strong ties to the Polish underground and Soviet army. They were responsible for protecting 200 Jews living in a forest encampment. Only 21, he was the youngest platoon commander. When the area was liberated by Soviet forces, he joined the Polish army. He survived the war."

Partial list of Jews in Kamionka-Strumilowa

Last name	First name	Gender	Disposition	Source
PASTERNAK	Yosef	M	Shoah	Yad Vashem
PASTERNAK	Yentl	F	Shoah	Yad Vashem
PASTERNAK	Towa	F	Shoah	Yad Vashem
PASTERNAK	Matel	F	Shoah	Yad Vashem
PASTERNAK	Bela	F	Shoah	Yad Vashem
PASTERNAK	Faigel	F	Shoah	Yad Vashem
PASTERNAK	Hencia	F	Shoah	Yad Vashem
PASTERNAK	Sonia	F	Shoah	Yad Vashem
PASTERNAK	Zlata	F	Shoah	Yad Vashem
PASTERNAK	Mirele	F	Shoah	Yad Vashem

PASTERNAK	Nachman	M	Shoah	Yad Vashem
PASTERNAK	Gitel	F	Shoah	Yad Vashem
PASTERNAK	Mania	F	Shoah	Yad Vashem
PASTERNAK	Sheindl	F	Shoah	Yad Vashem
PASTERNAK	Israel	M	Survived	Personal research
ADLER	Samuel	M	Shoah	Yad Vashem
ADLER	Basheva	F	Shoah	Yad Vashem
ADLER	Charna	F	Shoah	Yad Vashem
ADLER	Rachel	F	Shoah	Yad Vashem
ADLER	Wolf	M	Shoah	Yad Vashem
ADLER	Mordechai	M	Shoah	Yad Vashem
ADLER	Mina	F	Shoah	Yad Vashem
ADLER	Bina	F	Shoah	Yad Vashem
ADLER	Rechil	F	Shoah	Yad Vashem
ADLER	Mozes	M	Shoah	Yad Vashem
ACKERMAN	Yocheved	F	Shoah	Yad Vashem
ACKERMAN	Awraham	M	Shoah	Yad Vashem
ACKERMAN	Yakub	M	Shoah	Yad Vashem
AKSEL	Awraham	M	Shoah	Yad Vashem
BLACHMAN	Frank	M	Survived	Personal research
KOHEN	Rachel	F	Shoah	Yad Vashem
KOHEN	Abis	M	Shoah	Yad

				Vashem
KOHEN	Yehuda	M	Shoah	Yad Vashem
KOHEN	Cirel	F	Shoah	Yad Vashem
ROZEN	Malca	F	Shoah	Yad Vashem
ROZEN	Frima	F	Shoah	Personal research
ROZEN	Abish	M	Shoah	Yad Vashem
ROZEN	Peshe	F	Survived	Personal research
ROZEN	Feige	F	Shoah	Yad Vashem
ROZEN	Shmuel	M	Shoah	Yad Vashem
ROZEN	Mania	F	Shoah	Yad Vashem
ROZEN	Pesach	M	Shoah	Yad Vashem
ROZEN	Anna	F	Shoah	Yad Vashem
ROZEN	Peshe	F	Shoah	Yad Vashem
ALTMAN	Eidel	M	Shoah	Yad Vashem
ALTMAN	Nechama	F	Shoah	Yad Vashem
ALTMAN	Efraim	M	Shoah	Yad Vashem
ALTMAN	Oziyas	F	Shoah	Yad Vashem
ALTMAN	Yehuda	M	Shoah	Yad Vashem
ALTMAN	Esther	F	Shoah	Yad Vashem
ALTMAN	Yaakov	M	Shoah	Yad Vashem
ALTMAN	Eliezer	M	Shoah	Yad Vashem
ALTMAN	Gitel	F	Shoah	Yad Vashem

ALTMAN	Zeev	M	Shoah	Yad Vashem
ALTMAN	Yosef	M	Shoah	Yad Vashem
ALTMAN	Judith	F	Shoah	Yad Vashem
ALTMAN	Tziporah	F	Shoah	Yad Vashem
ALTMAN	Shmuel	M	Shoah	Yad Vashem
ALTMAN	Chana	F	Shoah	Yad Vashem
ALTMAN	Hadas	F	Shoah	Yad Vashem
ALTMAN	Dworah	F	Shoah	Yad Vashem
ALTMAN	Lazar	M	Shoah	Yad Vashem
ALTMAN	Aharon	M	Shoah	Yad Vashem
ALTMAN	Pinhas	M	Shoah	Yad Vashem
ALTMAN	Frieda	F	Shoah	Yad Vashem
ALTMAN	Nachman	M	Shoah	Yad Vashem

CHAPTER XI

UPDATED LIST OF JEWS THAT PERISHED IN THE AREA DURING THE SHOAH

This is a consolidated list of the martyrs with data from multiple sources. Although there is duplication with the necrology from the yizkor book proper, new data on each of these individuals has been added, increasing the amount of genealogical information available to researcher.

Legend for Source:
YB: Yizkor Book
P: Private letters and research
YV: Yad Vashem Pages of Testimony

Prepared by William Leibner

Last name	First name	Maiden name or nickname	Place of birth	Place of residence	Father	Mother	Gen	Spouse	Child	Source
AARON	Miriam			Jarczow	AARON		F			YB
AARON	Rachel			Jarczow	AARON		F			YB
AARON	Raphael			Jarczow	AARON		M			YB
ACKSTEIN	Zalman			Jarczow			M			YV
ADLER	Reuven			Jarczow			M			YB
ADLER	wife		Wichownik	Jarczow			F	Reuven		YB
AFTEWITZER	Haya Sheindel			Jarczow			F			YB
AFTEWITZER	Malka Breine			Jarczow			F			YB
AFTEWITZER	Riwkah			Jarczow			F			YB
AKSELRAD	Feige			Jarczow			F	Pessah	and mother	YB
AKSELRAD	Pessah			Jarczow			M			YB
AKSELRAD	son			Jarczow	Pessah	Feige	M			YB

Surname	Given Name			Town	Father	Mother	Sex	Spouse	Other	Source
ALBAUM	Bracha			Jarczow			F			YV
ALBOM	Josef			Jarczow			M			YV
ALTER	Moshe			Yidaliv			M			P
ALTMANN	3 sons			Jarczow	Yekil	wife	M		and family	YB
ALTMANN	Aaron			Yidaliv	Haim	Hinda	M			P
ALTMANN	daughter			Jarczow	Yekil	wife	F			YB
ALTMANN	Haim			Yidaliv	Shmuel	Peshe	M			P
ALTMANN	Hersh			Yidaliv	Haim	Hinda	M			P
ALTMANN	Hersh			Yidaliv	Shmuel	Taube	M			P
ALTMANN	Hinda	Hibel		Yidaliv			F	Haim		P
ALTMANN	Hudes			Yidaliv			F	Leizer		YB
ALTMANN	Leah			Yidaliv	Haim	Hinda	F			P
ALTMANN	Leizer			Yidaliv	Shmuel	Peshe	M			YB
ALTMANN	Peshe						F			P
ALTMANN	Peshe	Mandel		Yidaliv			F			P
ALTMANN	Shmuel			Yidaliv	Haim	Hinda	M			P
ALTMANN	Shmuel			Yidaliv	Leizer	Hudes	M			YB
ALTMANN	Shmuel			Yidaliv			M		and 3 sons	P
ALTMANN	Taube	Kurtz		Yidaliv			F			P
ALTMANN	Tzipe			Yidaliv			F	Shmuel	2nd wife	YB
ALTMANN	wife			Jarczow			F	Yekil		YB
ALTMANN	Wolf			Yidaliv	Shmuel	Taube	M			P
ALTMANN	Yehoshua			Yidaliv	Haim	Hinda	M			P
ALTMANN	Yekil			Jarczow			M			YB
ALTMANN	Yossef			Yidaliv	Shmuel	Taube	M			P
ANDEK	Bunem			Jarczow			M			YB
ANDEK	wife			Jarczow			F	Bunem	and children	YB
ARLENDER	Dudel			Jarczow			M			YB
ARLENDER	Esther			Jarczow			F	Zalmen	and 7 children	YB
ARLENDER	Haya Feige			Jarczow			F	Dudel		YB
ARLENDER	Israel			Jarczow			M			YB
ARLENDER	Itzhak			Jarczow			M			YB
ARLENDER	Riwtche			Jarczow			F	Israel	and 2 children	YB
ARLENDER	Tzipi			Jarczow			F	Itzhak	and 2 children	YB
ARLENDER	wife			Jarczow			F	Yossef	and 2 children	YB
ARLENDER	Yossef			Jarczow			M			YB
ARLENDER	Zalmen			Jarczow			M			YB
ASTERMAN	Blime			Jarczow			F	Meir		YB

Surname	Given name			Town			Sex			Source
ASTERMAN	daughter			Jarczow	Meir	wife	F			YB
ASTERMAN	husband			Jarczow			M			YB
ASTERMAN	Itche			Jarczow			M			YB
ASTERMAN	Meir			Jarczow			M			YB
ASTERMAN	Meir			Jarczow			M			YB
ASTERMAN	Ratzi			Jarczow			F	husband		YB
ASTERMAN	Simha			Jarczow			M			YB
ASTERMAN	Uri			Jarczow			M			YB
ASTERMAN	wife			Jarczow			F	Itche	and 2 children	YB
ASTERMAN	wife			Jarczow			F	Uri	and child	YB
ASTERMAN	wife			Jarczow	Meir	wife	F	Meir		YB
ASTERMAN	wife			Jarczow			F	Simha		YB
ASTMAN	Ethel			Jarczow		Hinde	F		and husband	YB
ASTMAN	Henia			Jarczow		Hinde	F			YB
ASTMAN	Hinde			Jarczow			F			YB
ASTMAN	Motel			Jarczow		Hinde	M			YB
ASTMAN	Shmuel			Jarczow		Hinde	M			YB
AUSTEIN	Beile			Jarczow			F			YB
AUSTEIN	Esther			Jarczow			F	Itzik	and 6 children	YB
AUSTEIN	Itzik			Jarczow			M			YB
AWRAHAM	Zishe's wife	Raci		Jarczow			F		and children	YB
BACH	Haim			Jarczow			M			YB
BACH	Rachel			Jarczow			F	Haim	and child	YB
BALTEN	Esther			Jarczow			F	Moshe	and 6 children	YB
BALTEN	Itzhak			Jarczow			M			YB
BALTEN	Moshe			Jarczow			M			YB
BARER	Haim			Jarczow			M			YB
BARER	Haim			Jarczow			M			YB
BARER	Hila			Jarczow			F	Haim		YB
BARER	husband			Jarczow			M			YB
BARER	Michael			Jarczow			M		and family	YB
BARER	Moshe			Jarczow			M			YB
BARER	Sarah			Jarczow	Haim		F	husband		YB
BARER	wife			Jarczow			F	Moshe	and child	YB
BARITZ	daughter			Jarczow	husband	Mindel	F			YB
BARITZ	daughter			Jarczow	Pithiya	wife	F			YB
BARITZ	Golde			Jarczow			F	Haim Wolf	and family	YB

Surname	Given Name			Town			Sex	Relation	Notes	Source
BARITZ	Haim Wolf			Jarczow			M			YB
BARITZ	husband			Jarczow			M			YB
BARITZ	Israel			Jarczow			M			YB
BARITZ	Lemil			Jarczow			M		family	YB
BARITZ	Mindel			Jarczow			F	husband		YB
BARITZ	Pithiya			Jarczow			M			YB
BARITZ	son			Jarczow	husband	Mindel	M			YB
BARITZ	Toibe			Jarczow			F	Israel		YB
BARITZ	wife			Jarczow			F	Yehezkel		YB
BARITZ	wife			Jarczow			F	Pithiya		YB
BARITZ	Yehezkel			Jarczow			M			YB
BAUM	Itzhak			Jarczow			M			YB
BAUM	wife			Jarczow			F	Itzhak	and children	YB
BAUM	wife			Jarczow			F	Wolf	and 3 children	YB
BAUM	Wolf			Jarczow			M			YB
BAUM	Yaakow			Jarczow			M			YB
BAUMAN	Henoch			Jarczow			M			YB
BAUMAN	Hersh			Jarczow			M			YB
BAUMAN	wife			Jarczow			F	Hersh	and family	YB
BAUMAN	wife			Jarczow			F	Henoch	and family	YB
BECK	Asher			Jarczow			M			YB
BECK	Benyamin			Jarczow			M			YB
BECK	daughter			Jarczow		Yente	F		and family	YB
BECK	Esther			Jarczow			F	Shalom	and family	YB
BECK	Haim			Jarczow			M			YB
BECK	Meite			Jarczow			F	Benyamin	and 4 children	YB
BECK	Shalom			Jarczow			M			YB
BECK	Tzirel			Jarczow			F	Asher	and 4 children	YB
BECK	wife			Jarczow			F	Haim	and 4 children	YB
BECK	Yente			Jarczow			F			YB
BEER	Dawid			Jarczow			M			YB
BEER	wife			Jarczow			F	Dawid	and 2 children	YB
BEINHOLTZ	Sarah			Kikizaw			F			YB
BELLER	husband			Jarczow			M			YB
BELLER	Yuta			Jarczow			F	husband	and 4 children	YB
BERENHOLTZ	Aaron			Kikizaw			M			YB

GaliciaYizkor Book

BERENHOLTZ	Mendil			Kikizaw			M		YB
BERENSTEIN	Hersh			Jarczow			M		YB
BERENSTEIN	Hershel			Jarczow			M		YB
BERENSTEIN	wife			Jarczow			F	Hersh	and family	YB
BERENSTEIN	wife			Jarczow			F	Hershel	and child	YB
BETIG	Miriam			Jarczow			F	Yossel	and 6 children	YB
BETIG	Yossel			Jarczow			M			YB
BIENSTOCK	Israel			Jarczow			M			YB
BIENSTOCK	wife			Jarczow			F	Israel	and 2 daughter	YB
BIGLER	Sera			Jarczow			F			YV
BILLER	Awraham			Jarczow			M			YB
BILLER	Elikum			Jarczow			M		and child	YB
BILLER	Helen			Jarczow			F	Itzhak		YB
BILLER	Itzhak			Jarczow			M			YB
BILLER	Mintche			Jarczow			F			YB
BILLER	Mintche			Jarczow	Shifra		F			YB
BILLER	Mordechai			Jarczow			F		and family	YB
BILLER	Mordechai			Jarczow			F			YB
BILLER	Ruchtche			Jarczow			F		and children	YB
BILLER	Sara Malka			Jarczow			F			YB
BILLER	Shifra			Jarczow			F			YB
BILLER	wife			Jarczow			F	Awraham	and child	YB
BLANKHAMMER	Aaron			Jarczow			M			YB
BLANKHAMMER	Brontche			Jarczow			F	Aaron	and family	YB
BLAUSTEIN	Eva			Jarczow			F	Yossef	and family	YB
BLAUSTEIN	Haim			Jarczow			M			YB
BLAUSTEIN	Henie			Jarczow			F	Haim	and 4 children	YB
BLAUSTEIN	husband			Jarczow			M			YB
BLAUSTEIN	Israel			Jarczow			M			YB
BLAUSTEIN	Mordechai			Jarczow	Zalmen	Sarah	M			YB
BLAUSTEIN	Sarah			Jarczow			F	Zalmen		YB
BLAUSTEIN	Sarah			Jarczow			M	husband		YB
BLAUSTEIN	son			Jarczow	Yossef	Eva	M			YB
BLAUSTEIN	son			Jarczow	Israel	wife	M			YB
BLAUSTEIN	wife			Jarczow			F	Israel		YB

BLAUSTEIN	wife			Jarczow			F	son	and 2 children	YB
BLAUSTEIN	wife			Jarczow			F	Yaakow	and 2 children	YB
BLAUSTEIN	Yaakow			Jarczow			M			YB
BLAUSTEIN	Yossef			Jarczow			M			YB
BLAUSTEIN	Zalmen			Jarczow			M			YB
BLICK	Baruch			Jarczow			M			YB
BLICK	Baruch			Jarczow			M			YB
BLICK	Blime	daughter of Rabbi		Jarczow			F			YB
BLICK	daughter			Jarczow	Feiwel		F			YB
BLICK	Deworah			Jarczow			F			YB
BLICK	Dworah			Jarczow			F			YB
BLICK	Feiwel			Jarczow			M			YB
BLICK	Hannah Bashe			Jarczow			F			YB
BLICK	Hersh			Jarczow			M			YB
BLICK	Idis			Jarczow	Hannah Bashe		F		and 3 children	YB
BLICK	Malka			Jarczow			F			YB
BLICK	Mordechai			Jarczow			M			YB
BLICK	Mordechai			Jarczow		Malka	M			YB
BLICK	Shmuel			Jarczow			M			YB
BLICK	Shmuel			Jarczow			M			YB
BLICK	Shmuel			Jarczow			M			YB
BLICK	wife			Jarczow			F	Mordechai		YB
BLICK	wife			Jarczow			F	Baruch	and child	YB
BLICK	wife			Jarczow			F	Hersh	and 2 children	YB
BLICK	wife			Jarczow			F	Baruch	and child	YB
BLICK	wife			Jarczow			F	Mordechai		YB
BLICK	wife			Jarczow			F	Shmuel		YB
BLOCK	wife			Pekalowicz			F	Yudel	and 2 children	YB
BLOCK	Yudel			Pekalowicz			M			YB
BLUTMAN	Jehoshua			Jarczow			M			YV
BLUTMAN	Kopel			Jarczow			M			YV
BLUTMAN	Rywka			Jarczow			F			YV
BRATTER	Awraham			Jarczow			M			YB
BRATTER	Ber			Jarczow			M		and children	YB
BRATTER	daughter			Jarczow	Shlomo	Ethel	F			YB
BRATTER	Ethel			Jarczow			F	Shlomo		YB
BRATTER	Freide			Jarczow			F		and	YB

									family	
BRATTER	Hersh			Jarczow			M			YB
BRATTER	husband			Jarczow			M			YB
BRATTER	Itche			Jarczow			M		and family	YB
BRATTER	Klaman			Jarczow			M		and family	YB
BRATTER	Mali			Jarczow			F	Awraham	and 3 children	YB
BRATTER	Malka			Jarczow			F		and family	YB
BRATTER	Meir			Jarczow			M		and child	YB
BRATTER	Meir			Jarczow			M		and child	YB
BRATTER	Mendel			Jarczow			M	and family		YB
BRATTER	Sarah	daughter of	Shlomo	Jarczow			F	husband		YB
BRATTER	Shlomo			Jarczow			M			YB
BRATTER	wife			Jarczow			F	Hersh		YB
BRATTER	Yossef			Jarczow			M		and family	YB
BUBER	Dawid			Yidaliv			M			YB
BUBER	Deworah						F	Itzhak		P
BUBER	Haya			Yidaliv			F		and 3 children	YB
BUBER	Itzhak						M			P
BUBER	Lea				Itzhak	Deworah	F			P
BUBER	Shmuel				Itzhak	Deworah	M			P
BUBER	wife			Yidaliv			F	Dawid	and 3 children	YB

CHAPTER XII

Bibliography

Pinkas Kehilot at Yad Vashem in Jerusalem

Archives at Yad Vashem in Jerusalem

Pages of Testimony at Yad Vashem in Jerusalem

Interviews with Klara Lowenkrown–Alter

Interviews with Karola Lowenkrown–Baum

Interviews with Regina Lowenkrown–Diengott

Interviews with Shmuel Lowenkrown

Interviews with Peshe Rozen Pasternak

Interviews with iSRAEL Pasternak

Interview with Dr. Aida Mudrik

Interview with Israel Pasternak

Interview with Tziporah Mizmor

Gerstel, Mordechai, Rabbi Dr. Khurban Yartchov in Yiddish.

Zuccotti, Susan: *The Italians and the Holocaust*, Basic Publishers Inc. New York. 1987.

Margherita, Marchione: *Did Pope Pius XII help the Jews?*, Paulist Press, USA.

Special thanks to all those that provided documentary and photographic materials that enabled the completion of the project.

Galicia Yizkor Book

INDEX

A

Aaron, 135, 225
Ackerman, 222
Ackstein, 135, 225
Adler, 135, 222, 225
Aftewitzer, 135, 225
Aksel, 222
Akselrad, 135, 225
Aktman, 36
Albaum, 226
Albom, 226
Alter, 38, 41, 42, 59, 226, 232
Alter-Lowenkrown, 42
Altholtz, 53, 54
Altman, 4, 5, 8, 10, 13, 14, 15, 16, 17, 18, 19, 22, 23, 24, 25, 26, 27, 28, 29, 30, 31, 32, 33, 34, 35, 36, 37, 38, 51, 53, 54, 55, 60, 103, 126, 168, 223, 224
Altman-Lowenkrown, 51
Altman-Mandel, 15, 30
Altmann, 56, 59, 60, 135, 136, 226
Altman-Pasternak, 13, 31
Altman-Rozen, 15, 30
Altman-Rozen-Pasternak, 31, 33
Amdin, 128
Amir, 15
Andek, 136, 226
Arlender, 136, 226
Ashkenazi, 83, 136
Asterman, 124, 136, 226, 227
Astman, 136, 227
Austein, 137, 227
Avishes, 111
Avramel, 117
Awraham, 137, 227

B

Bach, 137, 227
Bagdalio, 204
Balak, 127, 128
Balten, 137, 227
Barer, 137, 227
Baritz, 137, 227, 228
Barter, 137
Baum, 19, 38, 48, 61, 71, 103, 110, 111, 112, 123, 126, 137, 138, 228, 232
Bauman, 138, 228
Beck, 90, 138, 228
Beer, 138, 228
Beinholtz, 138, 228
Beller, 138, 228
Ben Ran, 15
Ber, 79
Berenholtz, 77, 228, 229
Berenstein, 138, 229
Berger, 138
Beryl the musician, 117
Betig, 138, 229
Bialik, 113
Bienstock, 4, 5, 15, 24, 27, 59, 138, 229
Bienstock-Altman, 5, 27
Bigler, 229
Biller, 138, 139, 229
Binstein, 122
Blachman, 220, 222
Blaichman, 220
Blaichman (Blachman), 220
Blankhammer, 139, 229
Blaustein, 139, 229, 230
Blech, 110, 115
Blick, 110, 111, 123, 139, 140, 230

Galicia Yizkor Book

Block, 78, 230
Blutman, 93, 230
Blutreich, 140
Boim, 102, 104
Botwin, 15
Bratter, 140, 230, 231
Breindel, 174
Brodsky, 129
Buber, 56, 60, 168, 231

C

Carozzi, 197
Chiam from Podliski, 79
Ciffer, 140
Cisterner, 140
Cohen, 15

D

Dawid, 140, 141
Deniwer, 141
Derniwer, 141
Diengott, 38, 49, 50, 60, 141, 232
Diwald, 141
Donner, 141
Dorf, 141
Doron, 15
Dreifuss, 141
Drucker, 141
Druker, 123
Dudie, 141

E

Eckhaus, 141
Ehrenwerrt, 141
Ehrenwert, 141
Eichenstein, 115, 141
Eichstein, 108
Einhorn, 103, 141
Eisensher, 141, 142
Epstein, 142

F

Fange, 80
Fanger, 80, 142
Fedder, 142
Feder, 142
Fefer, 93
Fehler, 122
Feivel from Podlisk, 122
Feler, 125
Felzner, 76, 77, 142
Fennik, 142
Feuer, 93
Figer, 15, 35, 36, 142, 143, 178, 179, 180, 181, 182, 186, 187, 188
Figer-Altman, 35, 36
Figer-Mismer, 179, 180
Figger, 60
Fingerhoit, 143
Finke, 143
Fir, 123
Fishman, 17
Flashner, 143
Fleher, 123
Flehr, 143
Fleisher, 143, 144
Fleishner, 144
Fligelman, 144
Fligelmann, 74, 169
Fogel, 144
Frenkel, 144
Fridel, 144
Friedman, 144
Friedmann, 144
Frostak, 19, 103

Galicia Yizkor Book

G

Gastenbauer, 144
Geitesman, 144
Gelber, 56, 144, 168
Ger, 124
Gerstel, 18, 19, 71, 74, 77, 78, 79, 80, 81, 83, 103, 104, 108, 110, 115, 126, 131, 144, 145, 167, 188, 232
Gerster, 109
Gerstl, 102, 104, 109, 110, 115, 131
Gerstler, 56
Gisser, 145
Giter, 56
Gitter, 168
Glatstein, 17
Gleisman, 93
Gold, 145
Goldshtecher, 145
Goldstein, 15, 145
Gootman, 129
Gordon, 15
Gorin, 17
Gottesman, 110, 115, 124
Gottesmann–Heller, 84
Gottlieb, 78
Greenstein, 35, 174
Greif, 64, 65
Grinwald, 145
Grits, 38
Gritts, 15
Gros, 145
Gross, 145, 146
Grosshtern, 146
Grubber, 168
Gruber, 56
Gutman, 194
Gutthertz, 146

H

Habercorn, 146
Hahn, 146
Haitches, 123
Haller, 117
Halpern, 120, 146, 147
Handelsman, 147
Hardes, 147
Hass, 147
Hasten, 43, 46, 56, 168
Hawa, 147
Haya, 147
Hecht, 147
Hersh from Kamenopole, 81
Herzl, 84
Hibel, 15, 59, 226
Hinda, 147
Hirschl, 212
Hirshorn, 147
Hitz, 123, 147
Hochberg, 71, 122, 147, 148
Hochberger, 167
Hochnerger, 167
Hodges, 38
Honik, 148, 149
Hopper, 3, 5
Horowitz, 115, 149

I

Indik, 86, 122, 149
Israel from Podlisk, 122
Itzhak, 149

J

Javitz, 128

Galicia Yizkor Book

K

Kac, 93
Kahane, 124, 149
Kaminka, 178
Kaminker, 109
Kanner, 149
Karfil, 123
Kassel, 149
Kassner, 149
Kastner, 149, 150
Katz, 38, 74, 110, 125, 150, 169, 170
Katzenelbogen, 83
Kaufman, 150
Kehr, 150
Keller, 81
Kenigsberg, 68
Ker, 125
Kerner, 125, 150
Kessel, 150
Kestler, 150
Kez, 150, 151
Kimmel, 123, 125, 151
Kirchner, 151
Klap, 19, 103, 126
Klapp, 151
Klein, 151
Klihiner, 123, 124
Knochn, 152
Kohen, 222, 223
Kolokoff, 3, 5
Kolokoff Hopper, 3, 5
Koningsberg, 152
Korfel, 152
Kórógyi, 177
Kraner, 152
Kraus, 212, 213, 214
Kreiner, 122, 152
Krepel, 120
Krieg, 56, 152, 168
Kristal, 152
Krumfer, 152
Kulikow, 179
Kuperberg, 152
Kupperman, 152
Kurtz, 15, 30, 57, 59, 168, 226
Kurtz-Altman, 15, 30

L

Lacher, 19, 103, 126, 152, 153
Lackman, 153
Laksan, 153
Landau, 153
Latt, 77, 153, 154
Latz, 154
Lavon, 15
Leibner, 1, 3, 7, 15, 61, 71, 135, 225
Leiter, 57, 168
Leon, 154
Lerner, 85, 86, 154
Lewenberg, 122, 123, 154
Lewenkron, 154
Lewenkrown, 40, 50, 168, 169
Libes, 154
Lieberman, 154
Linder, 57
London, 15
Lowenkron, 57, 60
Lowenkrow, 60
Lowenkrown, 4, 8, 35, 37, 38, 39, 40, 41, 42, 43, 44, 45, 46, 47, 48, 49, 50, 51, 54, 61, 70, 71, 86, 232
Lowenkrown-Alter, 232
Lowenkrown-Baum, 61, 71, 232
Lowenkrown-Diengott, 232
Lukas, 119, 120
Lustig, 93

Galicia Yizkor Book

M

Magnats, 129
Majer, 93
Mandel, 4, 8, 15, 30, 53, 54, 55, 56, 57, 59, 60, 61, 91, 154, 169, 178, 182, 188, 226
Mandel-Altman, 54, 55
Mantel, 74
March, 71
Marchione, 215, 232
Margoles, 78
Margolies, 78
Marinelli, 197, 198
Marsh, 154, 155, 167
Maszkowski, 73
Matalon, 15
Mehl, 155
Mehr, 80
Meilech, 155
Meisel, 155
Meizel, 125
Melamed, 111
Melnik, 124
Mendelowic, 61
Mendelowicz, 57, 61, 169
Messer, 155
Messinger, 209, 210
Metzger, 155
Milchiker, 81
Mimelman, 125
Mintzer, 155
Mismer, 4, 6, 8, 171, 173, 174, 176, 178, 179, 180, 182, 183, 184, 185, 188, 190, 191, 192, 193, 194, 195, 196, 197, 198, 199, 200, 202, 203, 204, 205, 206, 207, 208, 209, 210, 211, 212, 213, 214
Mismer-Messinger, 210
Mismer-Schlesinger, 209
Mismer-Zausmer, 174
Mizmer, 179
Mizmor, 205, 232
Mohrer, 67, 68, 69, 71, 74, 89, 155, 167
Morer, 19, 103, 126
Moshe, 155
Moss, 80
Most, 155
Mudrik, 232
Mukdoni, 17
Myers, 15

N

Nacht, 155
Nag'y, 178
Nash, 156
Neubauer, 43, 44, 45, 61, 156, 169
Norenstein, 94
Noubauer, 38

P

Papuy, 156
Pasternak, 13, 15, 31, 33, 34, 38, 49, 54, 218, 219, 220, 221, 222, 232
Pavelic, 178, 194
Peah, 122
Peshe from Lissak, 79
Pfennik, 156
Pilsudski, 85
Pinhas, 156
Potocki, 72
Pruchnik, 217
Putchnik, 156

R

Rabbi Abele, 115
Rabbi Mordechai, 71, 83
Rabbi Zeev-Wolf, 83
Rapaport, 83

Rapp, 156
Rappaport, 156
Rata, 156
Ratz, 156, 157
Reb Alter the Melamed, 122
Reb Yokali, 111
Reinard, 157
Reiner, 157
Reiser, 111
Reizer, 157
Rheines, 127
Rimfel, 117
Riwka from Winnik, 167
Rockberger, 1, 3
Rosen, 15, 57
Rosenberg, 157, 178
Rosenfeld, 83
Rosentzweig, 35
Roth, 157
Rothstein, 157
Rotshield, 129
Rozen, 13, 15, 30, 31, 32, 33, 57, 60, 61, 219, 220, 223, 232
Rozen Pasternak, 232
Rozen-Pasternak, 220
Rubin, 158
Rudnitzky, 15
Rundt, 94

S

Samet, 158
Samit, 77
Sanes, 111
Saphirshtein, 17
Sarfatti, 196
Sattler, 15
Schaffer, 158
Scharer, 158
Scherer, 15, 16, 17

Scherer-Altman, 17
Schidlowski, 158
Schlesinger, 209
Schlezinger, 208
Schnaper, 158
Schnapper, 158
Schneck, 158, 159
Schtapler, 78
Schuster, 159
Schvarz, 202, 205
Schvarz-Mismer, 202, 205
Schwartz, 15, 22, 35, 124, 159, 194, 207
Schwartzman, 38
Schwartz-Mismer, 207
Segal, 159
Shaeffer, 80
Shaerer, 159
Shamesh, 111
Shapiro, 159
Shehr, 19, 103, 126
Sheindele, 159
Sheptacz, 159
Sher, 159
Sherer, 22, 59
Sherer-Altman, 22
Sherryl, 15
Shmirer, 159, 160
Shneckbach, 160
Shneider, 79, 160
Shnerkel, 160
Shofer, 80, 160
Shorr, 122
Shoss, 160
Shoval, 35
Shpatz, 123, 160
Shpiesback, 79
Shraga, 160
Shrank, 160
Shtahl, 160

Galicia Yizkor Book

Shtarnebel, 124
Shteig, 160
Shteiner, 123, 160
Shtekel, 178
Shternberg, 160
Shtoltzberg, 77, 79, 160
Shtrang, 160, 161
Shtriker, 161
Shtrum, 35, 36, 38
Shubs, 161
Sigel, 161
Simmelman, 161
Sirop, 19, 103, 126, 161
Sobelman, 175
Soffer, 161
Soffres, 161
Spitzer, 178
Spritzman, 175
Stahl, 161
Stein, 161
Steiner, 161
Steller, 161, 162
Stern, 162
Stoltsberg, 19, 103, 126
Stoltzberg, 162

T

Tajg, 94
Talasowska, 162
Taube, 19, 103, 126, 162, 169
Teitelbaum, 162
Teneboim, 169
Tenenbaum, 57, 58, 61, 162
Tenevoim, 169
Teomim, 83
Tiberger, 35
Tiger, 162
Tile, 162
Tola, 162

Torn, 162
Traber, 162
Treiber, 162
Tremeiter, 117
Tritt, 15
Tzeiger, 162
Tzigler, 124, 162, 163
Tzuckerberg, 163
Tzwerling, 58, 169
Tzwetter, 163
Tzwetti, 163

U

Unger, 178

V

Vitalini, 197

W

Walla, 163
Waller, 163
Wander, 173
Warm, 163
Wasser, 163
Wassner, 74
Weintraub, 53, 56, 58, 60, 61, 163, 169, 178, 182
Weintruib, 61
Weissman, 122, 123, 163, 164
Weitzman, 15
Weizer, 164
Wellner, 164
Wertman, 164
Wiener, 164
Wilkenfield, 38
Winter, 164
Wissotsky, 129
Wolf the glazier, 124

Wolff, 164
Wortzel, 164
Wulfson, 15

Y

Yaacov from Podliski, 79
Yaakow, 164
Yaggid, 164, 165
Yartchov, 232
Yekel, 165
Yekil, 117
Yokel the Cantor, 114
Yona the musician, 117
Yossel, 165
Yudele, 165
Yudele from Podliski, 79

Z

Zalman the non-talker, 123
Zamzilig, 165
Zausmer, 173, 174, 175
Zausmer-Mismer, 173
Zaysner, 174, 175
Zhitomor, 84
Zilberstein, 165, 166
Zimmerman, 19, 103, 126, 166
Zinger, 166
Zitamor, 84
Zitzamer, 166
Zlatkes, 166
Zuccotti, 215, 232